Mike Wilkins

GLORY IN THE FACE

The Face of Christ and the Strength to Face Anything

Glory in the Face

Copyright © 2016 by Mike Wilkins

No part of this publication may be reproduced, distributed, or transmitted in any form or by any means, including photocopying, recording, or other electronic or mechanical methods, without the prior written permission of the author, except in the case of brief quotations embodied in critical reviews and certain other non-commercial uses permitted by copyright law.

"UNLESS OTHERWISE NOTED, Scripture quotations are from the ESV Bible (The Holy Bible, **English Standard Version**), copyright © 2001 by Crossway Bibles, a publishing ministry of Good News Publishers. Used by permission. All rights reserved."

OTHER VERSIONS CITED:

"NASB" *Holy Bible: **New American Standard Bible**.* © 1995. LaHabra, CA: The Lockman Foundation.

"KJV" *The Holy Bible,* **King James Version**. Cambridge Edition: 1769

NOTE: Underlined portions of biblical texts are solely the author's emphases.

Tellwell Talent

www.tellwell.ca

ISBN

978-1-77302-397-7 (Paperback)
978-1-77302-399-1 (eBook)

DEDICATED
to the **West London Alliance Church** family,
with my love and respect,

and to the memory and continuing fruitfulness of
Dr. John Owen and **Mr. Jonathan Edwards**,
who taught me what it means to see the face of Christ.

Psalm 84:5,7

Blessed are those whose strength is in you,
in whose heart are the highways to Zion.

… They go from strength to strength;
each one appears before God in Zion.

Table of Contents

Chapter 1:   STRENGTH ON PARADE 1

Chapter 2.   IN THE FACE OF PAIN 11

Chapter 3.   IN THE FACE OF CHANGE 25

Chapter 4.   IN THE FACE OF PEOPLE 47

Chapter 5.   THE FACE IN THE MIRROR 69

Chapter 6.   THE FACE OF CHRIST 87

Chapter 7.   IN THE FACE OF DEATH 109

Chapter 8.   GLORY ON PARADE 119

APPENDIX I 129

APPENDIX II 133

ACKNOWLEDGMENTS 135

ENDORSEMENTS 137

ABOUT THE AUTHOR 140

FOREWORD

Glory in the Face was the name of a sermon series before it became the title of this book: a series of sermons I preached on Sunday mornings in the fall of 2011, the particular autumn coinciding with my own fall from good health.

It was the set of sermons I had thought up—and thought through, and prayed about—on the 2011 version of my annual *First-Thing-in-the-Spring Solo Canoe Trip* in Temagami Provincial Park: five glorious days of silence and solitude, camping beside, and paddling on, lakes as still as glass and as cold as ice. It was an utterly breathless experience, and, as it turned out, the last solo canoe trip of my life.

The theme of the sermons: *finding the strength to face anything,* rendered the series more personally relevant and applicable than any group of sermons I had ever preached. Half-way through the preaching of the series, I learned that I needed a major surgery in order to save my eyesight. The final sermon of the set was preached three days prior to that surgery. My public announcement to the congregation gave a certain flare to the series' conclusion. The surgery itself was a delicate procedure requiring seven hours and two surgeons: a neurosurgeon and an otolaryngologist, which, being interpreted, means a "brain surgeon" and an "ear, nose and throat surgeon." After that came 25 days in the hospital, an eight-week absence from the pulpit, and a whole year of getting the hang of getting along without a pituitary gland.

Just as this medical adventure was winding down, a *real* health disaster was discovered; this one not in my attic but in my, um, basement. It was in fact exactly the problem I had spent the previous year being grateful to God that I *didn't* have. That is, in April, 2013, I was diagnosed with cancer. Of the colorectal kind. Thickening the plot a lot, the nasty thing had metastasized to my liver. It turned out that the whole pituitary business was not *The Thing* at all. It was only the dress rehearsal for *The Really Serious Medical Thing* that followed.

Another pair of doctors—both of them oncologists—recommended an 18-month treatment, featuring three rounds of chemotherapy; one with radiation. Each round was preliminary to one of three big surgeries which I evidently also required: the first in my, um, basement to remove the primary tumor, and the other two to remove—but I learned to say, *to resect*—three-quarters of my liver. When my wife and I asked for the "straight goods" in plain language, we were told that I had just a 10% likelihood of living long enough to complete the treatment. "Every one of these six things will have to go really, really well," one of the oncologists explained.

As you might imagine, since, prior to my skull surgery, I had never been seriously ill in my life, the church family prayed faithfully for me and for my doctors.

What happened next? The first two rounds of chemotherapy (the first with radiation), and the first two surgeries, went so surprisingly well that both the third chemotherapy and the third surgery were cancelled.

In June, 2014, I was declared "cancer-free." Happily, I explained the good news to the church. My cancer was "in remission," and

Foreword

there was only a 50:50 probability that it would come back. Ten months later, a CT-scan confirmed that it had.

These days, I am officially out of the pulpit, formally excused from pastoral leadership, living on Disability Insurance Benefits, and "permanently," but intermittently, receiving chemotherapy for what is now my incurable cancer. For a while (with only God knowing how long this "while" will last), I am living *with* cancer—and preparing myself to die *of* it.

My wife and I continue to attend the church's Sunday Morning Worship Services. Week by week, we worship our great and gracious God in the company of our church family, some of whom still think of me as their pastor, while others assume we are newcomers. Some of the latter group introduce themselves with assurances that we are going to love this church—but we already do. In my own mind, every Sunday morning I make an appearance as Casper the Friendly Ghost, happily haunting the premises, and taking great pleasure in observing for myself what became of the church after my work there was done.

For almost five years now, I have, by the grace of Jesus Christ, been finding the strength to face many uncertainties, a number of inconveniences, some pain, and the permanent loss of some things I have loved for many years. And I am continuing to find the strength to face the oncoming challenges of actually dying.

My *good* news is that these years have not been horrible. On the contrary, for me, and my magnificent wife, this experience has been loaded with the peace of God. Our minds and our hearts are guarded by it. And the joy of the Lord is our strength.

It does seem to me that the sermons I brought home from that last solo canoe trip—as much as I intended them to benefit the people to whom I would preach them—were God's gifts to me.

And now there is a book entitled *Glory in the Face*. It is written in the hope, and with the prayer, that what God revealed to me five years ago—and what I have learned by experience since then—*will* be a practical help to a number of people; some of whom I am never going to meet in this life. To them, and to the West London Alliance Church family, I say, "May the peace of God guard *your* hearts and minds in Christ Jesus. And may the joy of the Lord be *your* strength."

    Mike Wilkins
    London, Ontario
    Summer, 2016

Chapter 1: STRENGTH ON PARADE

in which we see people marching by

Paul, an apostle of Christ Jesus by the will of God ...
[2 Corinthians 1:1]

In September, 1984, three weeks before I turned 30 years old, I became the pastor of West London Alliance Church, a small congregation in a medium-sized city in south-western Ontario. To me, it was both a privilege and a challenge. The church and I were about the same age. As its ninth solo pastor, I took on the challenges that were the results of the varied ministries of the church's previous pastors: the growing pains and shrinking pains, the building projects and relocations, the financial challenges, the personality conflicts, and, I suppose, the various failures to adjust to any or all of the above. To add to that formidable list of challenges, I was, by far, the youngest pastor the church ever had hired.

All the same, being Pastor #9 seemed to me a privilege. I believed what I was told by the wise and godly man who pastored the Toronto church where I had been working. "Being as young and as inexperienced as you are," he had said, "you should not expect another opportunity as promising as this one." So I agreed to start, feeling honoured—and very eager not to mess this up.

From the beginning, one of my strategies for not messing up—and for not making a confused church even more confused about itself, and about its very young pastor—was to select a small number of past preachers and pastors, and to try diligently to follow their examples. By studying their biographies and journals, and their sermons, lectures, treatises, letters and other writings, I hoped to learn what they had learned about being a good and faithful pastor. I called them my Five Dead Men—one from each of the last five centuries. To remind myself that I was committed to learn from their wisdom, and to live accordingly, I hung framed portraits of them on my office walls. There was John Calvin from the 16th century; John Owen from the 17th; Jonathan Edwards from the 18th; Robert Murray M'Cheyne from the 19th; and Martyn Lloyd-Jones, who didn't die until 1981. Later, in an effort to be less narrow, I chose others, reinventing myself as a pastor with Nine Dead Men. On my list, and my wall, were added John Flavel, George Whitefield, Charles Spurgeon, and C.S. Lewis, who lived until I was nine years old. In time, I decided that too many focal points was too unfocussed, so I reduced and reworked the list, returning it to its original size. My Final Five are John Owen, Jonathan Edwards, Charles Spurgeon, G.K. Chesterton and C.S. Lewis. More than any of my other Dead Men, Dr. Owen and Mr. Edwards are the ones from whom I learned what the Apostle Paul wrote about "our hearts" shining with "the light of the knowledge of the glory of God in the face of Jesus Christ" [2 Corinthians 4:6].

I selected each of these men for the same reasons. In addition to success in not messing up, each was a man of sincere faith in God, intense love for the Lord Jesus Christ, (in most cases) definite knowledge of what the Bible actually teaches, consistent commitment to his own theological convictions, intellectual strength, moral integrity, and a good track-record of keeping in balance the

Strength on Parade

many responsibilities and privileges of being (in most cases) the pastor of a church, the faithful husband of a happy wife, and the godly father of children who grew up to love and respect him. No role model is perfect, of course. But for the years I pastored "West London," I benefitted from the instructions and the examples of these inspiring men, whose portraits still hang on my walls, and whose bodies lie still in their graves.

I sometimes envisioned these role models of mine, boldly, joyfully, thoughtfully, walking in a great parade. Intelligent, powerful, humble men of God, they marched with purpose for the years of their fruitful ministries. Each was positioned on the route in a particular part of the history of the church of Jesus Christ. Each provided me with a motivating example to follow.

I was clear from the start that each of these men had heroes of their own—fellow-participants in what they all knew to be the most significant movement in human history—all of them following the original 11 marchers in what was, at first, a very humble parade that began on a very small hill just outside of a very important city.[1]

> ... they returned to Jerusalem from the mount called Olivet, which is near Jerusalem, a Sabbath day's journey away ... Peter and John and James and Andrew, Philip and Thomas, Bartholomew and Matthew, James the son of Alphaeus and Simon the Zealot and Judas the son of James. All these with one accord were devoting themselves

---

[1] "The 11" were the original 12 apostles, minus Judas Iscariot. They were referred to as "the eleven" in the final chapters of Matthew, Mark and Luke, and in the first two chapters of Acts.

to prayer, together with the women and Mary the mother of Jesus, and his brothers.
[Acts 1:12-14]

It was a small parade when it began. But many people saw the marchers, and some dropped what they were doing to fall in step with them: men and women, children and youth, choosing to march so as to follow Jesus. Step by step, these marchers walked towards the parade's end, where they knew that Jesus would be standing, waiting to greet them when they arrived [Acts 7:55,56]. There, each marcher will see him face to face [1 John 3:2]—almost all of them for the first time—and some will hear him say, "Well done, good and faithful slave. You have been faithful over a little; I will set you over much. Enter into the joy of your master" [Matthew 25:23]. Some of them, perhaps, will say in response: "I love you, O Lord, my strength" [Psalm 18:1].

Twelve years before I became "West London's" pastor, I too joined the parade. I was 17 years old, and had just become convinced of two things. What I needed most urgently was a savior, and Jesus Christ is the only one. Earnestly committing myself to Christ, I stepped off the sidewalk and began to walk with his people. I have been "on the march" ever since—although sometimes distractedly, and at other times, lethargically. Along the route, I have been helped by more experienced marchers; some whom I met in real life; some who, like my Dead Men, marched long before me.

Very close to the front of the parade, there walked a man named Saul, known for many years as "Saul of Tarsus." He was a Jew. In fact, he was a Pharisee, which is to say: he was very serious about his Jewishness. He was so serious that he committed himself to the destruction of Christianity. The spectacular transformation of this man's life is well-known, and can be called, without exaggeration, world-changing. In his own words, he *had* been "a blasphemer, persecutor, and insolent opponent" of the first generation of Christians [1 Timothy 1:13]; but through a remarkable experience, his life was entirely re-directed, and he soon became known as "Paul, an apostle of Christ Jesus by the will of God" [2 Timothy 2:1]. Of all the faithful marchers in this parade, the Apostle Paul is, I think, the one most obviously set apart by God as an example to all who march behind him [1 Corinthians 4:16; 11:1; Philippians 3:17; 4:9; 2 Thessalonians 3:9; 1 Timothy 1:16]. Certainly, each of my Dead Men looked to him as a personal example of how to live for Christ.

The Apostle Paul's life and his New Testament letters have had a great impact on my own thinking and understanding, and on my outlook, my interests and my ambitions. That is why, for the three decades I was the pastor of a church, I maintained a particular interest in the details of Paul's accomplishments and thoughts; and how, in the face of many difficulties, he remained faithful to Christ.

At times, as I think about him—a well-trained student of the Scriptures, a compelling preacher, a remarkably intelligent teacher (who wrote the letter to the Romans!), a visionary leader—I wonder what was going through his mind when he was receiving, say, "the forty lashes less one" for the fifth time; or was being brutally "beaten with a rod" for the third time; or, for the third time, was shipwrecked; and "adrift at sea for a night and a day." Was he afraid, or even terrified, enduring those hardships? And what was going through his mind for those tense and awkward minutes when, to escape from a civil ruler intent on having him killed, he was "let down in a basket through a window in the wall" of the city of Damascus [2 Corinthians 11:24-33]? *Was* he afraid? Was he humiliated? Or was he actually amused by the awkwardness of it all?

Sometimes, I wonder if all the scar tissue, and the bruises produced by his many floggings and beatings, made each successive affliction more painful? Or did he grow accustomed to the pain? Did those long hours adrift at sea become increasingly dreadful as the 24 of them wore on? More to the point, I wonder if this remarkable man of faith was ever seriously tempted to change his mind about serving Christ—about staying in the parade. Did he ever, even just for a while, come close to quitting?

Wonderfully, whatever thoughts, feelings and temptations confronted Paul, he never quit. As his marching days were winding down, and he was personally nearing the finish line, he wrote to his young associate Timothy, "I have finished the race" [2 Timothy 4:7]. The fact is, he never did quit—happily for all of us who march behind him, and look to him for inspiration. And also happily for us, he was able to explain, in detail, how he endured.

"I can do all things through him who strengthens me," he wrote to one of the churches in his care [Philippians 4:13]: *all things* meaning "everything he was specifically called to experience as "a servant (or slave) of Christ"; *through him* meaning "through Jesus Christ."[2]

Helpfully, other statements in the New Testament reveal how he attained this strength from Christ. In the book of Acts, there are three detailed accounts of his remarkable initial encounter with Jesus Christ. Here's the Acts 22 version:[3]

> "I am a Jew, born in Tarsus in Cilicia, but brought up in this city, educated at the feet of Gamaliel according to the strict manner of the law of our fathers, being zealous for God as all of you are this day. I persecuted this Way to the death, binding and delivering to prison both men and women,

---

[2] In English translations of the New Testament, the same Greek word ["*doulos*"] is translated as "slave" or "servant" or "bondservant." Paul the Apostle used the word to describe himself in Galatians 1:10 and Titus 1:1.

[3] The other accounts of Paul's conversion are in Acts 9 and 26.

> as the high priest and the whole council of elders can bear me witness. From them I received letters to the brothers, and I journeyed toward Damascus to take those also who were there and bring them in bonds to Jerusalem to be punished. As I was on my way and drew near to Damascus, about noon a great light from heaven suddenly shone around me. And I fell to the ground and heard a voice saying to me, 'Saul, Saul, why are you persecuting me?' And I answered, 'Who are you, Lord?' And he said to me, 'I am Jesus of Nazareth, whom you are persecuting.' Now those who were with me saw the light but did not understand the voice of the one who was speaking to me. And I said, 'What shall I do, Lord?'
> [Acts 22:3-10]

This great and historic transformation began with a flash of light. Perhaps we can picture it. Out of the blue, one day about noon, without warning, a great light shone on the man with the license to persecute Christians. The light was so great that he was knocked off his feet, and blinded. Lying there on the road, he heard a voice that he did not recognize. It called him by name and asked him a very troubling question: "Saul, Saul, why are you persecuting me?"

In response, this man, now blind, and no doubt terribly troubled, answered the question with one of his own: "Who are you, Lord?" The voice responded by informing him of what must have been, under the circumstances, indescribably alarming: "I am Jesus of Nazareth, whom you are persecuting."

In confusion and despair (I would think!), Saul asked a second question—a very practical one: "What shall I do, Lord?" And Jesus of Nazareth, whom Saul evidently had been persecuting, matter-of-factly replied, "Rise, and go into Damascus, and there you will be told all that is appointed for you to do" [Acts 22:10,11]. Saul of Tarsus was helped to his feet and led by the hand to a house in Damascus, where somebody was waiting for him [Acts 9:12-19]. In the years to come, as his new life work progressed, he became known throughout the Empire by his Roman name "Paul," and as a slave (a bond-servant) of the Lord Jesus Christ, serving rather than persecuting Christ by serving rather than persecuting the people of Christ.

This Jesus, whom Paul served, once stood in Jerusalem's Temple and cried out to the crowd, "I am the light of the world. Whoever follows me will not walk in darkness, but will have the light of life" [John 8:12]. There is nothing to stop us from imagining that Saul of Tarsus, at the time a proud Pharisee, was there in the Temple, listening to those provocative words. Certainly, many Pharisees *were* present on the occasion [John 8:13]. At any rate, by the time Saul arrived in Damascus, he *had* seen the light that was Christ, and he believed that Christ *was* in truth the Lord: the giver of "the light of life."

When *we* find ourselves walking in darkness, we walk slowly. Cautiously, we walk with our hands out in front of us, feeling our way forward, fearing what we might be about to walk—or fall—into! But as soon as someone turns on a light, we walk differently. If it is a bright and certain light, we walk boldly, confidently, with strong and certain steps. So did the Apostle Paul. For three decades, believing Christ to be "the light of the world," Paul no longer walked "in darkness," but with "the light of life," and "in a manner worthy of the Lord, fully pleasing to him, bearing fruit in every good work and increasing in the knowledge of God" [Ephesians 4:1]. For those long years, he was "strengthened with all power, according to [Christ's] glorious might." He walked with "endurance and patience with joy, giving thanks to the Father." For God had qualified him "to share in the inheritance of the saints in light," had delivered him "from the domain of darkness," and had transferred him "to the kingdom of his beloved Son" [Colossians

1:9-14]. In the strength of the Lord, Paul stayed true to his calling, proving himself, in time, to be one of Christ's most persevering and productive preachers and apostles and teachers [2 Timothy 1:11]. With his own life enlightened by Jesus, Paul lived as a light shining in the particular darkness that was the Roman Empire of the first century [Matthew 5:14; Philippians 2:15]. Learning from him, and following his example, so have multitudes of other good and faithful slaves of Jesus—in that first century of the new era, and in all the centuries that followed. To this day, that parade marches on.

Chapter 2.   IN THE FACE OF PAIN

> in which we see there is more to pain than the hurting

> *... we do not want you to be unaware, brothers, of the affliction we experienced in Asia.*
> [2 Corinthians 1:3-10]

Late one morning, many years ago, in the days when I was a healthy young pastor, I stood for a few awkward moments at the bedside of a very unhappy man. The poor guy had a number of difficulties troubling him, and that day I was one of them. It was painfully plain to me that he didn't want me—or, presumably, any other clergyman—standing at the side of his bed. But his wife did. She had asked me to pay her ailing husband a visit, and I had agreed to, hoping I could be of some comfort and encouragement, at least to her. So there I stood, trying to be pastoral, that is, helpful, in the way a shepherd should be helpful to a sheep.

I spoke to this man about the purposes of God, and about how the knowledge of God's purposes—or even an awareness that God *has* purposes—strengthens us to endure the challenges of life. As I finished my presentation, he looked at me skeptically (but not at all sheepishly), and he asked, "Have you ever had a catheter, Mike?" I had to admit that I hadn't. But I could tell, from the look on his face, that my pastoral words might have been more convincing to him if I had.

All these years later, I am qualified to answer "Yes" to the catheter question. In fact, if I do say so myself, I am extremely qualified. I have had, by now, a plethora of catheters! More impressively I have experienced the insertion of a significant number of other medical implements into a number of other significant personal orifices. Call it bragging rights.

Over these last few years, my various medical experiences, especially the unpleasant ones, have enabled me, from time to time, to serve more credibly as a comfort to people going through their own challenges. At other times, I have also (or instead) been able to help the people who know and love the challenged ones. My experiences have taught me that pain can be a good thing—or at least, a thing that does some good.

To a lot of people, the most significant thing about pain is the most noticeable thing: it hurts. But people *can* get things wrong. The truth that pain hurts *is* significant. But there is always more to pain and suffering than that. This, the Apostle Paul knew. That is why one of the first things he wrote about, in the New Testament book we call 2nd Corinthians, is the affliction and suffering with which he had recently been burdened. "We do not want you to be ignorant, brothers, of the affliction we experienced in Asia" (that is, modern-day Turkey) [2 Corinthians 1:8].

Evidently, it was important to Paul that the Christians of Corinth knew that he, and his young associate Timothy, were having tough and painful times. But Paul was not looking for sympathy. As a preacher and apostle and teacher, he was convinced of the significance of personal affliction, and he intended to pass

In the Face of Pain

on what he knew to the people of this church he had started. For the years he had been serving Jesus, from the day of his adventure on the Damascus road, to the time he wrote this letter, he believed that, for the people of Christ, the details of our lives, all of the details—the painful and even the horrible ones—come into our lives precisely according to God's specific purposes. This was a very important part of Paul's understanding of God, and he very much desired that it would become the same for the Corinthians. Paul had probably known from childhood the connection between pain and the purposes of God, for it is built into the well-known Old Testament story of the man named Job.

Poor Job suffered greatly, as did Paul—except more so. Just like Paul, Job was clear on the fact that his afflictions were not accidents. At one of the many low points in his despair, Job said, "Naked I came from my mother's womb, and naked shall I return. The Lord gave, and the Lord has taken away; blessed be the name of the Lord" [Job 1:21,22].

When Job's wife asked him, "Do you still hold fast your integrity?" and then encouraged him to "curse God and die", Job replied, "You speak as one of the foolish women would speak. Shall we receive good from God, and shall we not receive evil?" The unnamed narrator notes: "In all this Job did not sin with his lips" [Job 2:9,10]. At a later point in Job's suffering, he said of God, "Though he slay me, I will hope in him… This will be my salvation" [Job 13:15,16]. Whatever his wife and friends understood by his bold words, we can see in them Job's plain acknowledgement that God is both able and willing to do whatever he is pleased to do, and that he does so for reasons of his own. Job himself was very clear about this, and had a number of ways of saying so. For example:

> But ask the beasts, and they will teach you; the
> birds of the heavens, and they will tell you; or

> the bushes of the earth, and they will teach you; and the fish of the sea will declare to you. Who among all these does not know that <u>the hand of the LORD has done this</u>? In his hand is the life of every living thing and the breath of all mankind. [Job 12:7-10]

Job *was* a remarkable man. The question about his suffering that he asked his wife is not one we would expect. But it seems that Job's understanding of God included the expectation that God sometimes, for reasons of his own, *is* pleased to bring "evil" into the lives of his people. The Old Testament Hebrew word translated "evil" is also translated "disaster" [as in Amos 3:6 and Micah 1:12], and "calamity" [as in Isaiah 45:7]. It does not necessarily connote "moral evil," and is therefore similar in meaning to the Greek word used by Paul and translated in English Bibles as "affliction."

It was perhaps a surprise to his friends, and his wife, that in the midst of his suffering, Job blessed the name of the Lord. But many centuries later, so did Paul [2 Corinthians 1:3,4 (See also Acts16:24,25)]. Surely, this is not a coincidence. Paul's heritage being what it was, he must have been aware of Job's good responses to bad experiences, and there is New Testament evidence that Paul was greatly influenced by what Job said.

Job *did* struggle to understand why God had burdened him with such afflictions. But he was sure that God was the ultimate cause of his troubles, and to some degree, he was confident that, having designed the suffering, God would eventually deliver him from it. This confidence he expressed with the words: "This will be my salvation." These words can be taken to mean: "My present afflictions have been planned by God to deliver (or rescue, or save) me from *all* earthly affliction."

So then why do we suspect that Paul developed his profound perspective on suffering, at least in part, from the example of Job?

In the Face of Pain

Because, fascinatingly, we find Job's words in Paul's letter to the church at Philippi: a letter he wrote from a Roman prison cell in which he was waiting to learn whether or not he was about to be put to death. Strikingly, he was not waiting in despair, or with his mind full of angry questions. In fact, he was waiting with joy:

> What then? Only that in every way, whether in pretense or in truth, Christ is proclaimed, and in that I rejoice. Yes, and I will rejoice, for I know that through your prayers and the help of the Spirit of Jesus Christ <u>this will turn out for my deliverance</u>. [Philippians 1:18-20]

A little bit of study reveals that Paul's confident words include a precise quotation of Job's words.[4]

In the opinion of some students of the Bible (and for what it is worth, I am one them), Paul was indicating, by quoting Job, that he viewed his own suffering as Job had viewed his all those centuries before. Paul believed that his personal suffering was a significant part of the story that God was telling through his experiences—and a purposeful part of the sequence of events by which God was delivering him from evil, regardless of whether or not he would soon be executed.

Job responded well to his difficult circumstances, but Paul's responses were better—not because he suffered less than Job (although it seems he did), but because he understood better than Job the nature and intentions of God. Job knew God was wise, and mighty, and possessed knowledge and understanding, and he believed that God had specific (albeit unrevealed) purposes for

---

[4] A "precise quotation," as translated into English from the *Septuagint*: the Greek translation of the Old Testament commonly used in the time of the apostles.

everything that occurred in the life of "every living thing." But Paul knew much more clearly than Job what some of those purposes were. And we, with centuries of hindsight, can also know what gave Paul this advantage.

Paul knew more about God than Job did because Paul knew Jesus. And Paul perceived that his own afflictions were divinely designed to equip him to model, and explain, to the Corinthian Christians how to experience the mercy and comfort of God in their own pain. This was the first thing he wrote to them about (after the conventional formal greeting):

> Blessed be the God and Father of our Lord Jesus Christ, the Father of mercies and God of all comfort, who comforts us in all our affliction, so that we may be able to comfort those who are in any affliction, with the comfort with which we ourselves are comforted by God. For as we share abundantly in Christ's sufferings, so through Christ we share abundantly in comfort too. <u>If we are afflicted, it is for your comfort and salvation;</u> and if we are comforted, it is for your comfort, which you experience when you patiently endure the same sufferings that we suffer. Our hope for you is unshaken, for we know that as you share in our sufferings, you will also share in our comfort. [2 Corinthians 1:3-7]

So here we find the Apostle Paul, a faithful and exemplary slave of Christ, marching courageously along his difficult section of the parade route, steadied and comforted by the knowledge that God was using his suffering to direct and benefit these followers of Christ. And there is more!

Before turning his attention to other matters of interest and concern, Paul made note of a second purpose of God that he could see was built into his personal pain. Paul could see that another of God's intentions was to lead him and Timothy to a greater reliance on him.

> We were so utterly burdened beyond our strength that we despaired of life itself. Indeed, we felt that we had received the sentence of death. But <u>that was to make us rely not on ourselves but on God</u> who raises the dead. He delivered us from such a deadly peril, and he will deliver us. On him we have set our hope that he will deliver us again.
> [2 Corinthians 1:8-10]

Even after two long decades of serving Christ, Paul was still in training—even on the most basic matter of relying on God. Even at this late point in Paul's life, God was still bringing productive perils into his life. Paul's faith was still being stretched and strengthened.

Personally grasping this difficult but plainly-stated truth should bring us to see—or to see more clearly—how the details of our own lives also are accomplishing God's purposes. Whether our circumstances are pleasant and comfortable, or unpleasant and painful, God has his purposes.

With Paul (and other New Testament heroes), and with Job (and other Old Testament heroes), as our examples, we should think about what we can do to better our understanding of God's purposes for us. Comparing the experiences of Job and Paul, we can see that Paul's better response to affliction came from his better knowledge of the nature of God, especially as God's nature is revealed in Christ. And here we come to a practical question; one *so* practical that we will take it with us as we continue our progress through 2nd Corinthians. The question is, **What can we do to know Christ better and so be strengthened to face anything?**

This first answer to this practical question aligns itself with the question that Saul of Tarsus asked that day that Jesus introduced himself. Lying on the road, blind and frightened, Saul asked in his helplessness, "Who are you, Lord?" The immediate answer he received from the Lord Jesus marked the beginning of the new life, and the new life work, that God had planned for him; the new life that Christ came into the world to provide—a life to be centred on knowing Christ [John 10:10; 17:3].

What makes this practical question *so* important, and sets us up to understand its first answer, is that becoming strong enough to face every challenge of life depends on truly knowing Christ— and truly knowing Christ begins with understanding the Bible. To become as strong as we will need to be, we must acquire a deep and practical knowledge of Christ that is grounded on a good understanding of what the Bible actually says. The obvious way to gain this understanding is to diligently read, and methodically study, the books of the Bible. Of course, regularly hearing the Word preached and taught, in the company of fellow-followers and worshippers of Christ—a privilege every member of a New Testament-styled church should experience—will be a significant help in this quest.

In Paul's case, it seems, acquiring a personal knowledge of Christ through the Scriptures began by his learning to understand differently the Old Testament Scriptures he had been taught as a child, and had studied as a Pharisee. Later, he almost certainly gained specific insights—some, no doubt, startling insights—from his various interactions with the original apostles [e.g. Galatians 1:15-19; Acts 15:22,25,26]. We know that Paul also received unique and miraculous revelations from Christ himself [1 Corinthians 15:8; 2 Corinthians 12:1-7]. Through these experiences, and quite possibly others of which we have not been told, God equipped Paul to serve the churches of God as an apostle of Christ—and also to write about half of the 27 "books" of the New Testament!

Paul's new relationships, to Christ, to the Apostles, and to some of the first churches of Christ, uniquely provided him with many answers to the question of *who* the Lord is. For us, and for all who march behind Paul, the completed Bible is ours to read and study and contemplate. And we *should* devote ourselves to doing so, for as Jesus himself once stated, the Scriptures "bear witness" about him [John 5:39]. And so the first answer to our practical question is, **Learn as much about Christ as we can from diligent reading and study of the Bible.**

A simple and obvious place to begin studying the Bible is Matthew, Mark, Luke and John: the four "Gospels." Each of these documents provides us with a vast amount of information about the words, the wisdom, the works and the character of Jesus. Learning the Gospels is a good beginning. But there are 62 other books of the Bible which also can play a part in revealing to us specifically who Jesus is.

There is, of course, the entire Old Testament. Book by book, as different as they are from each other, we can discover real-life (albeit partial) portrayals of Jesus, as his character, his intentions and his interests are reflected in the lives and actions of various people in Bible history.

In Genesis, for example, we meet Isaac, the begotten son of Abraham (not the *only* begotten son, but *that* is another story). Isaac was the child that God had promised Abraham—a son through whom the whole world was to be blessed [Genesis 12:1-3; 22:15-18]. Mysteriously, Abraham offered up this promised son, whom he greatly loved, as a sacrifice to God, in specific obedience to God's instruction. Then this father received back his son [Genesis 22:2,9-12; Hebrews 12:17-19], which surely should bring to our minds a certain other father, and the sacrifice he made of his only begotten son [John 3:16; Galatians 3:16].

As another example of how better to know Christ from a study of the Old Testament, we can read of Solomon, the son of King David. Once he had inherited his father's throne, Solomon built for God the temple that his father David had desired to build. For a while, Solomon was the wisest of all men, and the most glorious of all kings [1 Kings 10:23,24]. For those good years, he presented the people of his time, and, eventually, the Bible-readers of all times, with a real-life, real-time representation of the ultimate "Son of David" [Matthew 1:1], who, many generations after Solomon [Matthew 12:42], lived and died and rose again to build his church [Matthew 16:18]—the church of Jesus Christ referred to, by the Apostle Paul, as "God's temple" [1 Corinthians 3:16].

The books of the Old Testament tell the history of the people of God, and the long and complicated story of God's dealings with them. In seeking to know all we can about Christ, we can learn that the lives of many of God's people are foreshadows, mysteriously (but, of course, imperfectly) previewing the One promised by God from the beginning of the human story [Genesis 3:15]. Paul taught the Corinthians, in his previous letter, to understand the Old Testament in this way, and to look for Christ, and to "find him," in his many Old Testament manifestations (admittedly some not as obvious as others) [1 Corinthians 10:1-11]. Christ can be better known, and more deeply loved, by an understanding of the Scriptures that bear witness about him; not only as the dearly-loved son being sacrificed by his father, and as the wise and glorious king building a temple for God as his father wished, but also as a unique sort of bread that came from heaven to feed God's people; the ark of the covenant that God established with his people; the bush that was burning without being consumed; and the desert rock from which God's people could drink to preserve their lives.

Returning to the New Testament, along with the four Gospels, we can explore the 23 other sacred writings that God has given to us through the minds, the words and the obedience of certain men,

In the Face of Pain

including Paul, who spoke "from God as they were carried along by the Holy Spirit" [2 Peter 1:21; 3:15,16]. These Scriptures reveal to us yet more of who Jesus of Nazareth actually is. Diligently reading and studying the New Testament, we are enabled to more completely answer that first and most fundamental question of Saul of Tarsus.

Finally, there is the mysterious book of Revelation, uniquely able to acquaint us more deeply with Christ. With its own now-difficult style, it reveals Jesus as he was never revealed before. No longer is he dressed in the clothes of a first-century Middle East carpenter or rabbi. Here he is revealed in images that expand and deepen our understanding of him.

I should say personally that for the first dozen years of my life as a Christian, I devoted very little attention to this last New Testament book. It seemed to me to have been written in code—and there I was, two thousand years later, an eager Bible student without a "decoder" card, or any sort of decoding secret. I was eventually led out of this darkness by the startling announcement (all good news to me) that the "decoder," by which the book of Revelation can be understood, *has* been found. Except, it had never been lost. Shockingly, and strangely, it had always been right there in front of me. The secret key to understanding the last book of the New Testament, as it turns out, is the Old Testament. The mysterious, and obviously symbolic, images filling the pages of the Revelation are almost all Old Testament images, especially from Leviticus, where the altars, the offerings and the work of the priests are explained; from Daniel, with its strange beasts coming up out of the water; from Isaiah, with the new heavens and the new earth and the re-created city of God, and from Zechariah, with the gold lampstand and the two olive trees and those horses of colour. What a surprise!

By the time I moved to London, I was giving some serious attention to the book of "the revelation of Jesus Christ, which God gave him to show to his servants the things that must soon take place" [Revelation 1:1]. And I began to see Jesus in many new ways.

I saw him standing in the middle of seven golden lampstands—a priest clothed in a long robe with a golden sash. His face was shining like the sun, in full strength. His eyes flamed like fire. His voice sounded like the roar of many waters [Revelation 1:12-20].

I saw him coming down from heaven as a gigantic messenger of God (the Greek word translated as "angel" means "messenger"), wrapped in a cloud, with a rainbow over his head. Again, his face was shining like the sun, and his legs were like pillars of fire. He stood with one foot on the sea and one on the land, and he was calling out with a loud voice. He sounded like a lion roaring [Revelation 10:1-3]. I saw him seated on a white cloud, with a crown of gold on his head and a sickle in his hand [Revelation 14:1-4]. And I saw him as a conquering king seated on a white horse. Somehow, he was wearing many diadems. Somehow, a sharp sword was coming from his mouth [Revelation 19:11-16].

As much as these depictions of Jesus are mysterious, difficult to visualize, and, for many people, difficult even to appreciate, they *are* revelations given to us by God. Heavy with meaning, these depictions of our Lord Jesus Christ are given that we might know him better, and, with the eyes of our hearts [Ephesians 1:18], might see him more clearly. With these, and the other depictions of him in the Revelation, our Lord Jesus makes himself known to those who will humble themselves in reverence, and who will obediently study the Scriptures. At the very least, the book of Revelation compels us to stop only picturing Jesus as he lived for those few years in the world, dressed humbly in carpenter's garb, or in a rabbi's robe—his power, his majesty and his glory veiled, and hidden from our eyes.

By "abiding" in the Word, as Jesus phrases it, we will "know the truth," and the truth will set us free [John 8:31,32]. Free from the penalty and power of sin, of course, but also free from the serious

In the Face of Pain

perils of living without understanding the One who came into the world that we might have eternal life, and "have it abundantly" [John 10:10]. If we continue to grow in our knowledge of Christ, we will increasingly "taste and see that the Lord is good" [Psalm 34:8], and, as his good and faithful slaves, we will learn the details—even the enigmatic details—of how his goodness is embedded in every aspect of our lives.

So let us diligently read and study the Bible, and regularly have the Bible preached and taught to us. As it pleases him to do so, God *will* give us "ears to hear," and a mind that understands. God *is* able to open our eyes, healing us of our spiritual myopia, and enabling us to see how God uses the details of our lives—even the painful details—to accomplish his purposes and plans for us.

Paul understood by experience that one of the reasons that "knowing Christ Jesus" is a privilege of "surpassing worth" [Philippians 3:8] is that knowing him strengthens us to face life's afflictions. A thousand years before Paul began to experience this strength, King David of Israel was thanking God for it. David wrote:

> I love you, O LORD, my strength. The LORD is my rock and my fortress and my deliverer, my God, my rock, in whom I take refuge, my shield, and the horn of my salvation, my stronghold.
> [Psalm 18:1,2]

What Paul knew, that David did not, was that the *name* of the Lord his God—who *was* his strength—was "Jesus." So, as explicitly as the Apostle Paul prayed for the people in his charge, we can pray—for ourselves and for the people we know and love—that our great God, by his glorious grace—and in the powerful name of the Lord Jesus—*will* open the eyes of our hearts, enabling *us* to see "wondrous things" [Psalm 119:18]: especially, the many wondrous things that Christ Jesus has accomplished on our behalf, and the many wondrous things that Christ himself *is*.

> ## A PRACTICAL QUESTION:
>
> What can we do to know Christ better and so be strengthened to face anything?
>
> *"Who are you, Lord?"*
>
> 1. Learn as much about Christ as we can from diligent reading and study of the Bible. (John 5:39)

Chapter 3.   IN THE FACE OF CHANGE

> in which we see that sometimes God says, No.
>
> *Do I make my plans according to the flesh, ready to say "Yes, yes" and "No, no" at the same time? As surely as God is faithful, our word to you has not been Yes and No.*
> [2 Corinthians 1:16-20]

I give full credit to my 20th century Dead Man, C.S. Lewis, for what sometimes I am discredited for, that is, being strangely comfortable with the mostly-uninterrupted routines of my life. It is true that, in the last few years, my personal circumstances have changed greatly. But for me that has meant replacing one set of unchanging routines for another. Lewis has been my inspiration. Evidently, he was once asked by an interviewer if he found his life monotonous: for example, tutoring undergraduate students at the same university, in the same college, for twenty-nine years. "I like monotony," Lewis answered.

I plead guilty to the same affection. Partly from inborn quirkiness (I admit it), but also in deliberate imitation of this particular hero of mine, I have learned to enjoy saying that I like monotony, too. For that reason, there is to me no real mystery in my long stay at the first church that ever asked me to be its pastor. But there *is* a story in my staying for 30 years—I mean, rather than 20 years or 40.

The general notion with which I arrived at West London Alliance Church was that there was nothing much to be said in favour of pastoring a church for only a handful of years. This 32-year old church required its ninth pastor just because so many of my predecessors seem not to have agreed with me on that point. So I arrived at the church in 1984 with a general idea of staying for a good long while. My definite commitment to stay for a specific number of years came to me one day four years later. The specific number was 20.

I was out on a country road on one of my regular early morning runs, walking for a bit, and feeling free to do so because I was not, at the time, training for a race. Some years before, I had learned that the difference between a runner and a jogger (and between a serious runner and a runner who takes random walk breaks) is a filled-in and mailed-off Entry Form, especially a Marathon Entry Form. But I had not signed up for a race since I had moved to London, so a walk break had become a common occurrence. What *was* unusual about that particular break was that, as I walked, I complained to God about what seemed to me the disappointing results of my first four years at the church.

"Four years!" I exclaimed, as if there were someone listening who didn't know that already. All that preaching. All that teaching. All those church services. All that pastoral counseling. All that vision-casting. All those Elders' Meetings. And so little to show for it! With God as my witness, I lifted my eyes to the heavens and poured out my complaint. "Oh God," I cried. "I have given my life to this church!"

As I walked on, I thought about those words. I could almost see them, suspended in the air above me, like a caption printed over the head of a comic strip character. And then I began to *feel* like a comic strip character. New words came to me, and I said them out loud, too. But this time I was talking to myself. "What a twit you are, Wilkins! … 'Given your life to this church'! Really?"

Warming to the topic, I went on. "For four years—four measly years—you've been paid a decent salary to do the work you love (except for the Board Meetings). A measly four years! And you've been very healthy, mostly happy, generally appreciated, often thanked, and always paid. And you complain? And you dress up your complaint as some great sacrifice? And you complain to *God*!!! What a twit you are!"

Walking along that country road, I asked God to forgive me for my whining, my ingratitude—and my audacity. As I resumed running, it occurred to me that, although what I had said was unreasonable, and under the present circumstances even outrageous, it *would* be a fine thing, some day—many years in the future—to be *able* to say that I *had* devoted my life to this church, or to *some* church, should the West London elders ever decide to show me to the city limits. Perhaps for being a whiner. This line of thinking kept up with me as I made my way back into our neighborhood, and as I walked up the street where we lived. By the time I reached our driveway, I had settled on a definite number. "What I need," I said, as I untied my shoes, "is a 20-year plan."

Why *that* number? I had two reasons. In the first place, 20 years seemed an undeniably long time: five times longer than I had been there already. Secondly, in 20 years I would be in my fifties, which to me, at the age of 34, was an *unimaginable* thing. And so began the development of my "20-year plan."

Two decades later, I was well on into my fifties. I had pastored the church for two dozen years, and now had a second 20-year plan—two additional decades at the same church. For now, what seemed entirely unimaginable was to choose to start all over again at some other church. And by then, I pretty well loved every aspect of my life as this church's pastor, even the Board Meetings! Besides, I still had not crossed off my "To Do List" some of the things that were a part of my original 20-year plan. Turns out, some plans are more complicated to fulfill than you might think.

So I stayed at the church, and stayed busy with the important and gratifying work that God had given me to do there, with the intention of just keeping at it for a grand total of 40 years (which, as everyone knows, is a more biblical number than 20 or 30.)

In my days as a university student, a favourite English professor of mine sometimes quoted his father, who apparently liked to say, "Things always happen when you least expect them the most." I thought of that statement, when just after I turned 57, unexpected things began to happen to me, and many of the routines of my life began to change. It started with the discovery that my head was not only filled with many old theological convictions, and some new church ministry ideas, but also with a tumor (specifically, a pituitary macro-adenoma) that evidently needed to be surgically removed. Almost exactly a year later, I was dealt the Cancer Card. This larger, and more deadly, challenge brought me a whole new series of changes, along with the permanent loss of many of the things I had loved the most—running on country roads early in the morning, for example; and being the long-time pastor of a church.

The next big thing that the Apostle Paul wrote about in his second letter to the church of Corinth was the troublesome changes in *his* circumstances. He had recently failed to pay the Corinthians a visit he had promised them. Actually, he had promised them two visits: the first on his way to Macedonia, and the second on his return.

His stated intention was to lead them in a "second experience of grace" [2 Corinthians 1:15,16]—whatever he actually meant by *that* interesting phrase. Apparently, the Corinthians were very pleased with his plan. Certainly, they were displeased when the plan fell through. In their displeasure, they accused Paul of vacillating; interpreting his failure to visit as an indication of his unreliability and his lack of integrity. To them, his failure was evidence that he had made his plans "according to the flesh" [2 Corinthians 1:17].

To Paul, these were serious charges. He knew he was a slave of God, and he was not the sort of person who was "ready to say 'Yes, yes' and 'No, no' at the same time" [2 Corinthians 1:17]. What made the church's charges even more serious was that he was *more* than God's slave. He was also "an apostle of Jesus Christ, for the sake of the faith of God's elect … God, *who never lies*" [Titus 1:1,2]. So Paul found himself in the awkward position of defending his own integrity to one of the churches that he himself had established. Many of its members had first heard the gospel because Paul had travelled to Corinth to preach it. Many of them had became rooted and grounded in the gospel because Paul had stayed in Corinth for a year and six months to teach the Word of God [Acts 18:1-11]. As awkward as it was for him, Paul knew what he had to do to keep these troubled (and, in some cases, troublesome) Corinthian Christians established in their faith. So he did it. He came to his own defense:

> Our boast is this, the testimony of our conscience, that we behaved in the world with simplicity and godly sincerity, not by earthly wisdom but by the grace of God, and supremely so toward you. For we are not writing to you anything other than what you read and understand and I hope you will fully understand—just as you did partially

understand us—that on the day of our Lord Jesus you will boast of us as we will boast of you.
[2 Corinthians 1:12-14]

Then, perhaps just because he *had* invested 18 months in teaching them the Word of God, Paul attempted to further their understanding of the Lord Jesus Christ and the faithfulness of God:

> As surely as God is faithful, our word to you has not been Yes and No. For the Son of God, Jesus Christ, whom we proclaimed among you, Silvanus and Timothy and I, was not Yes and No, but in him it is always Yes. For all the promises of God find their Yes in him. That is why it is through him that we utter our Amen to God for his glory.
> [2 Corinthians 1:18-20]

The murmurings of the Corinthians are easy to imagine. "How can he say that his word 'has not been *Yes* and *No*'? Is not *Yes* and *No* exactly what his words *were*? And how does he dare link *his* vacillating to God's faithfulness?" These were not unreasonable questions, even if they were asked impertinently. But what Paul was saying, I think, is that, as unpredictable to us as the outcome of any of our own plans might be—however well-intended our plans are—what actually does occur in anyone's life is always in keeping with the will of God. In other words, being the Lord, the Creator and the Sustainer of all things, God has ordained the actual details of all our experiences. These details correspond precisely to the "plot line" of "the drama" that was written by God, and is being directed by the Holy Spirit—the drama that is now "on stage" in this "glorious theatre" we call the Universe.[5]

---

5 Credit where credit is due. William Shakespeare penned the metaphor of the world as a stage, in *As You Like It*, Act Two, Scene 7. John

In the Face of Change

So then everything that takes place in every person's life *is* the will of God. Sort of.

Many questions are raised by this startling idea of the sovereign will of God! Some of these questions are so loaded with unsettling implications, that some people—even some serious students of the Bible—rule out all discussion of this idea. I have interacted with people of that mindset from the time I began to include the topic in my Bible teaching. Many years ago now, with the help of my Dead Men, I had come to what I still believe is a better approach to these mysterious and even unsettling doctrines. Since those days, my approach was to accept all of the Bible as the Word of God, and to study even the difficult passages of the Bible seriously. I have learned to humble myself before the Lord, keeping always in mind the two truths that he is God, and that I am not. Charles Spurgeon once said in a sermon:

> I bless God that there are some things in the Bible which I never expect to understand while I live here. A religion which I could perfectly understand would be no religion to me; when I had mastered it, it would never master me. But to my mind it is a most delightful thing for the believer to bow before inscrutable mysteries, and to say, "My God, I never thought that I was infinite, I never dreamt that I could take thy place, and understand all things; I believe, and I am content.

Calvin referred to the whole created order as a theatre, for example, in Chapter 5, Section 8 of Volume I of his *Institutes of the Christian Religion*: "… *the greater part of mankind, enslaved by error, walk blindfold in this glorious theatre…*"

I have learned, in my study of the Bible—and been helped, both personally and pastorally—to differentiate between the two distinct meanings of the phrase "the will of God." This differentiation is of real importance, for there are many instances in the Bible where the phrase "the will of God" refers to the *laws* of God, that is, God's imperative statements of his moral expectations of us. For example:

> <u>This is the will of God</u>, your sanctification: that you abstain from sexual immorality.
> [1 Thessalonians 4:3]

> Give thanks in all circumstances; for <u>this is the will of God</u> in Christ Jesus for you.
> [1 Thessalonians 5:18]

On the other hand, there are texts in which the same phrase, "the will of God," refers to God's *plans*: his own designs by which he sovereignly works out the specific details of the life that each of us is living.

> Paul, an apostle of Christ Jesus <u>by the will of God</u>…
> [2 Corinthians 1:1]

A very challenging theological concept repeatedly stated in the Word of God is that in regard to both meanings of the phrase, "the will of God" is *always* "good and acceptable and perfect" to God—but in two different ways. Therefore, sometimes (oftentimes in fact), an actual historical occurrence is—from God's perspective—*both* good and *not* good.

The ultimate—and most stupendous—example of this sort of apparent contradiction is the execution of Jesus Christ. The people responsible for his crucifixion: Herod the king, Pilate the governor, certain Gentiles, and some of "the peoples of Israel," working together (more-or-less spontaneously), put Christ to death by committing many dreadful and inexcusable acts of disobedience to God. Every one of these horrible actions was completely contrary to the moral will of God, that is, God's *laws*. But *by* those lawless acts, these wicked people collectively accomplished God's specific intentions for mankind, exactly carrying out what "his hand and <u>his plan</u> had predestined to take place" [Acts 4:24-28]. In other words, what was done by Herod the king, the governor Pilate, and those other evildoers, was *not* good, or acceptable, or perfect. And yet, being exactly what God himself had planned, every one of their insults, humiliations and cruelties *was* good and acceptable and perfect as a part of the accomplishment of what God had ordained. It had all been prophesied more than 700 years before:

> [Jesus] was despised and rejected by men; a man of sorrows, and acquainted with grief ... Yet it was <u>the will of the LORD</u> to crush him.
> [Isaiah 53:3,10] (See Psalm 22, also.)

All that lawlessness was the will of God. The sacrifice was offered. The propitiation was accomplished. The powers of sin and of death were defeated. The devil and all his demons were undone. Certain men intentionally violated the will of God—and, as they did so, the will of God was perfectly fulfilled.

What many plain statements in the Bible make clear about the history of the human race, about the nature of being human, and, of course, about the nature of God, is to some well-intentioned Christians both unthinkable and impossible to believe. But the truth of God's complete control of all of life is set out plainly throughout the Scriptures. For example, in the Proverbs, we read:

> The plans of the heart belong to man, but the answer of the tongue is from the LORD.

> The LORD has made everything for its purpose,
> even the wicked for the day of trouble.
>
> The heart of man plans his way, but the LORD
> establishes his step.
>
> The lot is cast into the lap, but its every decision is
> from the LORD.
> [Proverbs 16:1,4,9,33]

Here, in one chapter of the Bible, is clearly set out a mind-stretching truth. God manages, and always has managed, *all* the details of human experience. "The answer of the tongue is from the Lord." The actual words we speak were ordained by God. So are the moves that everyone of us makes. "The heart of man plans his way, but the LORD establishes his step." Even in regard to the apparently "random" occurrences of life—even the *deliberately* random occurrences—in every case, "every decision is from the Lord." We can flip a coin, or roll dice, or draw straws, or, according to the equivalent ancient practice, we can cast lots. But always the same truth pertains: "every decision is from the Lord." And it is by no means only four verses in the book of Proverbs that say so. Throughout the entire Bible, the idea of randomness is flatly denied, and—as difficult and counterintuitive as it can seem—the concept of God's personal control of all that occurs is explicitly stated.

To the Colossian Christians, Paul wrote about Christ being not only the One who creates "all things," but the One who *sustains* all things as well.

> "… by him all things were created, in heaven and
> on earth … and <u>in him all things hold together</u>."
> [Colossians 1:16,17]

In the Face of Change

Similarly, the writer of the letter to the Hebrews declared the same spectacular details of Christ's direct involvement in our world, and the entire Universe:

> In these last days he has spoken to us by his Son, whom he appointed the heir of all things, through whom also he created the world. He is the radiance of the glory of God and the exact imprint of his nature, and <u>he upholds the universe</u> by the word of his power.
> [Hebrews 1:2,3]

Repeatedly, the Old Testament narratives state that the actual outcome of a particular event was specifically what God had ordained. One such story pertains to the disastrous reign of King Rehoboam. The foolish young king, having inherited his throne from his father, King Solomon, "abandoned the counsel that the old men gave him and took counsel with the young men who had grown up with him and stood before him." The writer then explained that "the king did not listen to the people, for <u>it was a turn of affairs brought about by the LORD that he might fulfill his word</u>, which the LORD spoke by Ahijah the Shilonite to Jeroboam the son of Nebat" [1 Kings 12:8,15].

Similarly, in 1st Chronicles, we read of a war that occurred in the days of King Saul. It was a fierce and deadly conflict between the valiant men of the tribes of Reuben, Gad and Manasseh and a large army of enemy warriors. Although these three tribes of Israel[6] were greatly outnumbered, "they prevailed over them, the Hagrites and all who were with them were given into their hands, for they cried out to God in the battle, and he granted their urgent plea because they trusted in him … many fell, because <u>the war</u>

---

6   To be precise, the story involves 2½ tribes of Israel. Manasseh was a "half-tribe."

was of God_" [1 Chronicles 5:18-22]. Not only in military battles, but in all aspects of life—corporate, individual, major and seemingly minor—the final answer to the question of *why* something worked out the way that it did is that God planned it that way. In the days of King Hezekiah, a great spiritual renewal of interest in the worship of God came about with surprising suddenness. The chronicler explained that "the service of the house of the LORD was restored. And Hezekiah and all the people rejoiced because God had provided for the people, for the thing came about suddenly" [2 Chronicles 29:35,36].

In view of God's absolute control of all things, the New Testament book written by "James, a servant of God and the Lord Jesus Christ," offers guidance. Regarding every single thing his readers have in mind to do, James wrote:

> Come now, you who say, "Today or tomorrow we will go into such and such a town and spend a year there and trade and make a profit"—yet you do not know what tomorrow will bring. What is your life? For you are a mist that appears for a little time and then vanishes. Instead you ought to say, "If the Lord wills, we will live and do this or that." As it is you boast in your arrogance. All such boasting is evil.
> [James 4:13-16]

Both scientists and historians pursue their work—and seek to understand the world in which we live—according to the principle that every action, and every event, is the effect of a particular cause. The biblical view of the natural world, and of humanity, is that God himself, infinitely wise, holy, just and good, is the "first cause," or the "prime mover," of all things. And what could be more reassuring than this? Even when we cannot comprehend how such and such a thing could ever have happened, or what

God could have possibly been thinking in bringing such a thing to pass, nonetheless:

> The LORD brings the counsel of the nations to nothing; he frustrates the plans of the peoples. The counsel of the LORD stands forever, the plans of his heart to all generations.
> [Psalm 33:10,11]

Whether an actual event is, to our minds, good and acceptable and perfect, or not the least bit good, *entirely* unacceptable, and *totally* imperfect, the Word of God teaches us that God is good and that what God does is good [Psalm 119:67]. "Righteousness and justice are the foundation of his throne" [Psalm 97:2]. Accordingly, God speaks to us these words of assurance:

> My thoughts are not your thoughts, neither are your ways my ways, declares the LORD. For as the heavens are higher than the earth, so are my ways higher than your ways and my thoughts than your thoughts.
> [Isaiah 55:8,9]

The Lord God Almighty rules the world, and no one can stop him from doing what he intends to do. "Whatever the LORD pleases, he does, in heaven and on earth, in the seas and all deeps" [Psalm 135:6].

I have learned that when you "get the hang" of looking at such statements in the right way (that is, in the way that is consistent with all that the Bible says on the subject of who is actually in charge of this world), there is tremendous comfort and peace to be experienced. The Lord Jesus once said that "even the hairs of your head are all numbered" [Matthew 10:31]. I like to think that what Jesus was saying was something more marvelous than that the hairs of each particular human head have been accurately counted. In itself, that fact *is* worth noting. But it seems to me that the word "numbered" implies something like a serial number engraved on a material object—a bicycle, for example—to distinguish it from similar objects. Surely the Lord was not talking just about hairs, but about all of the details of life. Surely he was referring even to the seemingly incidental details; even the details we are inclined to complain, and perhaps sulk, about—thinning hair, a thickening waist, or both, for example. Surely the point of the Lord's striking statement is that all of the details of our lives are packed full of the purposes of God.

Some philosophers and scientists, evidently, have theorized that a butterfly fluttering its wings can cause a hurricane thousands of miles away. In a similar vein, certain medieval theologians are reputed to have speculated about the number of angels that can simultaneously dance on the head of a pin.[7]

But we who take seriously the plain and, in some cases, puzzling statements of Scripture do well to reflect on just how many of the purposes of God might be built into any one event in any one part of anyone's life.

The Lord Jesus clearly taught that even apparently incidental events, and even seemingly insignificant details of life, are in fact ordered by God the Father, according to his wise and righteous design. How obvious is it then that there are divine intentions in such significant events as the suffering of Job. Regardless of

---

[7] Two "Scholastics" of the Middle Ages, Thomas Aquinas and Duns Scotus, are often named as the main "culprits" in what is now generally considered a good illustration of the pointlessness of theological speculation. But what these two brilliant scholars *were* exploring, among many metaphysical questions, was the intersection between the physical aspects of space and the nature of non-material spiritual beings.

whether or not Job, or his wife, or any of his friends, ever were able to discern something good, acceptable or perfect in the horrifying changes in his circumstances, his remarkable words stand. "The Lord gave, and the Lord has taken away; blessed be the name of the Lord" [Job 1:22].

Many centuries after Job had completed his role on the world stage, the Apostle Paul played his part. Trusting God enough to continue to obey him, he faced his share of trials, tribulation and pain. Some of his experiences came upon him suddenly and without explanation, for example, those that made it impossible for him to visit the Corinthians again (and again.) What is remarkable is that Paul never lacked the strength to face his troubles with peace and joy. Plainly, he believed that "God was working all things for the good of those who love him and are called according to his purpose" [Romans 8:28]. *All* things!

With that same conviction, Paul explained to the Corinthians that "the Son of God, Jesus Christ was not Yes and No"—that is, that Christ was not himself vacillating in carrying out God's plan—because God's plan, carried out "in" Christ, is "always Yes" [2 Corinthians 1:19]. In other words, under the sovereign control of the Lord Jesus himself, everything in life *does* go according to the plan of God. This, I think, is what Paul meant when he wrote: "For all the promises of God find their Yes in him. That is why it is through him that we utter our Amen to God for his glory" [2 Corinthians 1:20].

Throughout the centuries, people who have believed in the sovereignty, wisdom and goodness of God have expressed the peace and joy that *they* experienced through *their* faith in him. Jeanne-Marie Bouvier de la Motte-Guyon (1648-1717), a French woman now commonly known as Madame Guyon, was one such person. Imprisoned by the Roman Catholic Church on charges of heresy, she was very evidently strengthened for the ordeal by her relational knowledge of Christ. There in prison Madame Guyon wrote poems to express the confidence she was finding in the Lord—and the inner freedom she experienced for the *years* she lived in a dark, underground cell. Here are three verses from one of her best known:

> A little bird I am,
> Shut from the fields of air,
> And in my cage I sit and sing
> To him who placed me there;
> Well pleased a prisoner to be,
> Because, my God, it pleases thee.
>
> My cage confines me round;
> Abroad I cannot fly;
> But though my wing is closely bound,
> My heart's at liberty;
> For prison walls cannot control
> The flight, the freedom of the soul.
>
> O it is good to soar
> These bolts and bars above!
> To him whose purpose I adore,
> Whose providence I love;
> And in thy mighty will to find
> The joy, the freedom of the mind.

Another woman of similarly remarkable faith in God was Sarah Edwards, the wife of one of my Five Dead Men. At the age of 54, Jonathan Edwards died; his unanticipated death apparently the result of a smallpox inoculation. In a letter she penned to one of their daughters, Mrs. Edwards displayed the same peace and joy of which the Apostle Paul—and Madame Guyon—wrote. Like theirs, her soul was anchored by the truth that God has his "holy and good" reasons for all that occurs. It was theology that she had learned from her husband's faithful preaching of the Word of God:

> My very dear child,
>
> What shall I say? A holy and good God has covered us with a dark cloud. Oh that we may kiss the rod [that is, the rod of God's authority and discipline and correction], and lay our hands on our mouths. The Lord has done it. He has made me adore his goodness, that we had [your father] so long. But my God lives; and he has my heart. O what a legacy my husband, and your father, has left us! We are all given to God; and there I am, and love to be.
>
> Your ever-affectionate mother,
> Sarah Edwards.

We all have challenges. Some of them are brought about by unlooked-for changes in our circumstances—some that may seem unlucky, unfair or inexplicable. But God *does* have his reasons, whether or not we think we can see what they are. It might be difficult for some of us to accept the notion that God establishes our steps. But the Bible teaches us that God has, as it were, written the script by which our lives play out. It was apparently not a difficult thing for King David to believe. In one of his psalms, he said to God: "The days that were formed for me—every one of them—in your book were written—when as yet there was none of them" [Psalm 139:16].[8]

---

8 I have "re-ordered" the four phrases of this verse in an attempt to more clearly give its sense.

Glory in the Face

Things happen. Circumstances change. But, as it has been said (well, *sung*, actually), "You can't always get what you want." This is true, even when what we want is, in itself, clearly—even undeniably—a fine, fine thing. (A fourth consecutive decade of pastoral ministry at the same church, for example.)

According to my own long-held, fondly-cherished—and then suddenly-cancelled—plans, at the age of 70, and the conclusion of my 40 years of West London leadership, I was going to begin one more decade of service to God. My idea was to step down from my preaching responsibilities before I became dangerous—or an embarrassment to my family—reinventing myself as an author. My plan was that, working under the watchful eye of a theologically-sound editor, who would be neither aging or dangerous, I would remain busy, productive and happy for yet another ten years, until I reached the unimaginable age of 80.

Things *do* happen. Circumstances *do* change. As it turns out, I am almost certainly not going to live to be 70. In fact, I have it under good authority that living to 65 is now a long shot. Contrary to my own well-intentioned and (as I always thought) well-laid plans, I am *not* going to get what I want. I have become a real-life demonstration of a *Rolling Stones* song. But, by the grace of God, and according to his good and acceptable and perfect plan, I *am* a man who loves God. Therefore, evidently, I am "called according to his purpose." So I *do* get what I need [Romans 8:28,32].

The Bible is clear. The worshippers of Jesus Christ get everything they need. We get everything we need to serve him. Certain good works *are* being prepared for us, and *we* are being prepared for them. For we are God's "workmanship, created in Christ Jesus for good works, which God created beforehand that we should walk in" [Ephesians 2:10]. As each of us march along our particular section of this very long parade—our eyes wide open—God provides us, "according to his riches in glory in Christ Jesus" [Philippians 4:19], with everything required. Everything! That includes the strength to face every change in our circumstances, and the grace to wait patiently for that day when the Lord Jesus reveals to us the particular ways in which it *was* "good and acceptable and perfect" that we did not get everything we wanted.

What I have personally observed is that we do not always need to wait for such an explanation. Sometimes, we can discern for ourselves, at least in part, why we did not get what we wanted. I think I see now why God denied me that fourth decade. His reason—if I am getting this right—goes back to the audacious complaint with which I began my long-term planning. "I have given my life to this church," I had whined. I see now that God ordained for me three decades of pastoral work. Not two decades. Not four. Three. Then my assignment was terminated, and he gave me a new one. It was the last thing I was expecting, but he *is* God. He is able to do that.

Of course, my change of assignment would be a very different sort of thing if I were not going to die some time anyway. But I see that if my dying and death take place about now, instead of several decades from now, the people who have called me their pastor—some for a lot of years—will be able to see for themselves how I manage my share of end-of-life challenges. As West Londoners, they have heard me say from time-to-time, "Everyone is a good example of something." It's an adage that my most faithful pastoral colleague and I think we made up, 30 years ago when we were both just beginning our ministries. Quite obviously, my new assignment is to be a good example of how to die. Passing the assignment will mean dying in a way that pleases Christ, and that demonstrates trust in him. Alternately, blowing this assignment will mean I became a good example of how *not* to die.

I am quite sure that my new gig should *not* be called "dying for my church." It has never been *my* church, and it *was* died for thousands of years before it began, of course, by an *infinitely* better man. Nor should my assignment be called "giving my life for this church," as in, "First I gave my life *to* this church; now I am giving my life *for* this church." That would also be an extremely twit-ish thing to say. But I do think it is acceptable to the Lord for me to say that, having served the church family for many years by providing them with some sort of an example of how to live, I have now been called to show them for a few years an example of how to die.

I am sure of one thing. If I do manage to avoid messing this up, Christ himself will deserve the credit, as he gets the credit for this unexpected assignment itself. As with Job, and as with Paul, God did not ask for my permission. But he is supplying me with the strength I need to deal with the details he has written into my life-and-death story.

While I thank the God and Father of Jesus for the strength that he supplies, I am happy to conclude this chapter by giving Charles Haddon Spurgeon the final words. He emerged on the London, England church scene—at the age of 19!—as a startlingly dynamic preacher of the gospel of Christ. Not yet 20 years old, he was solidly grounded in the biblical theology of the Puritans of the 17th century, and profoundly devoted to Jesus his Savior. He preached from his church pulpit in London, and frequently throughout Great Britain, for almost 40 years (!), leading many thousands of listeners, both churchgoers and otherwise, to faith in Christ.

In his book of daily devotions he entitled "Morning and Evening," Spurgeon wrote plainly (for the Morning Reading of August 5) about the courage-building implications of Romans 8:28:

> Upon some points a believer is absolutely sure. He knows, for instance, that God sits in the center of the vessel when it rocks most. He believes that an invisible hand is on the tiller, and that wherever providence may drift, God is steering it. That reassuring knowledge prepares him for everything

… He knows too that God is always wise, and knowing this, he is confident that there can be no accidents, no mistakes and that nothing can occur that ought not to happen. He can say, "If I should lose everything, it is better that I should lose it than keep it if it is God's will. The worst disaster is the wisest and the kindest thing that I could face if God ordains it" … The believer's heart is assured, and <u>he is learning to meet each trial calmly</u> when it comes.

    Faithfully serving his Lord in the work of the gospel, Spurgeon persevered, in the early years, through a great deal of brutal criticism, both from the media of his day, and from theologically liberal church leaders. Much later in his long ministry, in what became known as the "Downgrade Controversy," he publically confronted what he saw as the deadly theological apostasy of his Baptist colleagues. Subsequently, he suffered yet more scorn and insult. All the while, for the 38 years of his pastoral ministry, along with many other kingdom endeavors, he humbly and quietly endured a daunting trio of extremely painful physical ailments. Several written accounts reveal that, at the age of 57, Charles Spurgeon met his final "trial"—dying in pain—"calmly." Calmly! As if he were fully prepared. Calmly. As if he had specifically been strengthened for it.

Chapter 4. IN THE FACE OF PEOPLE

in which we see that sometimes the problem is the people

But I call God to witness against me—it was to spare you that I refrained from coming again to Corinth. ... For I made up my mind not to make another painful visit to you. For if I cause you pain, who is there to make me glad but the one whom I have pained? And I wrote as I did, so that when I came I might not suffer pain ...
[2 Corinthians 1:23-2:5]

Really? "It was to spare [them] that [Paul] refrained from coming again to Corinth." Paul wrote as he did, so that when he came to Corinth he "might not suffer pain." *Really?* The fact is that, in Paul's day, that church was *that* kind of church. No one knew it as well as Paul. Under the circumstances, it was remarkably gracious of Paul to write to them so comforting and loving a letter—in fact, to write to them at all! In the space of seven sentences (that is, six verses), Paul used the words "pain," "affliction" and "anguish" eight times!

All the same, Paul assured these people that he was working with them for their joy [2 Corinthians 1:24]; that he expected they would make him glad [2 Corinthians 2:2]; that he felt so sure of them all that, when all was said and done, his joy would be their joy, too [2 Corinthians 2:3]; and that, in despite of the affliction, the anguish, and the many tears they had caused, his love for them was "abundant" [2 Corinthians 2:4]. The people of the church in Corinth may have been troublesome—and may have been to blame for how complicated their relationship with him had become—but Paul really did love them.

When I was half-way through high school, I was planning my life around the idea of avoiding having to work directly with people. In those days, I admired and agreed with the wisdom of Linus Van Pelt, my favourite character in my favourite newspaper comic strip [*Peanuts*, by Charles M. Schulz]. Linus was depicted on a popular poster, in those groovy days when posters were pinned or taped to almost every bedroom wall. This poster quoted him as saying: "I love mankind. It's people I can't stand."

That was my outlook, too. Working part-time, for two-or-three-month stints, at two hardware stores and a toy store, and finding that I did not enjoy the experience as much as I thought I would, I came to the settled conclusion that I was simply not suited for the sort of work that involved interaction with people. I was 15 years old, which seemed to me plenty old enough to have a few things all figured out. "Working with people is just not me, man," I explained to friends who I knew were old enough to appreciate my self-awareness. Having always been fond of dogs and cats, I decided to become a veterinarian. It felt good to have the whole matter of a career plan settled, even before I started driving, or shaving. With great satisfaction, I reflected on the personal advantages my new choice of profession offered. A very pivotal advantage, of course, was the obvious freedom from working with other members of the human race. With all of this settled, I returned my attention to performing in high school musicals, planning the next out-of-town ski day, along with playing road hockey, watching television, and—for several weeks before exams—studying a bit.

And then a couple of thoughts occurred to me. Firstly, my four-legged clients could not reasonably be expected to arrange their own transportation to my clinic. Secondly, even if some particularly gifted dog or cat did find its way to my door, it would almost certainly be unable to pay my fees. These, I could see, were significant issues.

By the time I was 18 years old, and a university student majoring in "pre-vet" biology, I had fully grasped the truth that these two obstacles compelled me to reconsider my future. So did the incidental fact that I turned out to be a very bad post-secondary biology student. Consequently, halfway through my second year of university, I transferred out of the Science Faculty, resetting my sights on a degree in English Literature. The switch was, in the first place, a matter of academic survival, but I was very aware that this change of direction meant I was almost certainly going to have to work with people after all.

Time has a way of changing a young man, and God has many ways. Picture me then, ten years later. I was in my late twenties, happily married, thrilled to be the father of one child, with another on the way—and longing for nothing more than to become the pastor of a congregation of people. My strong desire was to be the spiritual leader of a group of actual human beings: real people who would expect me to be, to some degree, an active part of their lives, as a flock of sheep expects to be cared for by a shepherd. The short explanation of this great change of heart is that God had poured into it a love for him; a love that produced in me a desire to help people in a significant and definite way. As the Book says:

> ... God's love has been poured into our hearts through the Holy Spirit who has been given to us.
> [Romans 5:5]

> We love because he first loved us.
> [1 John 4:19]

By then, I had lost touch with almost everyone who had known me in my teens. But how surprised they would have been if they heard that I was now longing to become a pastor. *"Really?"* I could imagine them saying. "Aren't pastors supposed to *like* people?"

It is a good question. As it turned out, my pastoral experience allowed me the delightful privilege of shepherding, and "doing church" alongside, many admirable, intelligent, godly, and likable people. But, at the same time, my years of being a pastor confirmed that, in church work, as in all of life, while liking people is generally a good thing, it is not an essential thing. This, in itself, is a good thing, in that sometimes liking people becomes an impossible thing. But certainly, it *is* required of a pastor—and of all Christians, actually—to *love* people, regardless of where they place on the Likability Scale. Alas, Linus's compelling philosophy could no longer be mine.

Besides loving God whole-heartedly [Mark 12:30], all who have entrusted their lives to Jesus are commanded to love people—and in three specific ways. For starters, we are all under orders to love our neighbors *as we love ourselves* [Mark 12:31]. The Greek word translated "neighbor" indicates proximity, even temporary proximity. So the good Samaritan lovingly and sacrificially cared for a man he "just happened" to find lying half-dead on the side of a road. Being even temporarily near to him, the Samaritan was obligated to think of the mistreated man as his neighbor. So, as an example to us all, he loved him *as he loved himself* [Luke 10:29-37]. In other words, the practical—and probably life-saving—love that the man from Samaria put into action was just what he himself would be hoping for, if ever he were mistreated so badly.

The second specific "love commandment" concerns other believers in Christ. Our orders are to love "one another" *as Christ has loved us*. That means we are to love our Christian brothers and sisters sacrificially—even if it seems that it might kill us to do so. The familiar tale of a soldier throwing himself on an exploding grenade to save the lives of his buddies is a very "Christian" story [John 13:34,35; 1 John 3:16]. Most of us will never have the opportunity to be so heroic. But if we keep our eyes (and hearts) open, we will all see opportunities to "lay our lives down"—in love—for a brother or sister.

Thirdly, and most counter-intuitively, we are also directed by the Lord Jesus to love our enemies *by doing good to them, by blessing them, and by praying for them*—even if they actually hate us, curse us, or abuse us [Luke 6:27,28].

In summary, whether or not we *like* the people we encounter, Christ commands us to love them. It is simply what we are under orders to do. And these strict orders are from our Savior, the person who reconciled us to God by *his* death while we were *his* enemies [Romans 5:10].

Towards the end of the first year of my new life as an actual church's pastor, I was encouraged and emboldened by a new friend who already had five years of pastoral experience. He is a few years older than I, but he was still a young man when we met. In one of our first conversations—to encourage me—he said, "I have been called worse things as a pastor than I was ever called as a hockey player." I was still enough of a rookie to be surprised by these words, but he said them with a smile, and concluded them with a wholehearted laugh. So I laughed too. In the many years that followed that happy conversation, his words, and his laugh, *did* encourage me to keep on loving the people I was pastoring—even the unlikable ones.

Back in those early days, whenever the parade brought me into close contact with "problem people," and I found myself out of step with them, I reminded myself that when I moved to London at the age of 30, it was not to play hockey.

From time to time, I *was* criticized, and even insulted, by people who seemed to find *me* very unlikable. At times, the criticisms felt severe. In some instances, some seemed rather creative—even imaginative. But, of course, there were occasions when I could see that the criticisms I received, regardless of how they were communicated, were warranted. As with some of my recent medical procedures, being helpful can mean being hurtful. In any case, God kept be mindful that I was a slave of Christ: "a man under authority" [Matthew 8:9]. I had my orders.

A very great distance ahead of me, both on the parade route, and in spiritual maturity, walked the Apostle Paul. In his complicated relationship with the Corinthian Christians, he has served me well as a good example of how I am called to behave when interacting with complicated people. Most of *us* are also complicated, I suppose, which explains why many of our relationships are something other than straightforward and simple. But the relationship that Paul, our good example, had with the Corinthians was less complicated than it *would* have been if, say, he were occasionally given to outbursts of anger, or was often grumpy, or was not very committed to consistently obeying Christ. Paul knew he was under strict orders to love those people—and he knew about love! It was he who had written (to *that* church!) these (now famous) words:

> Love is patient and kind; love does not envy or boast; it is not arrogant or rude. It does not insist on its own way; it is not irritable or resentful; it does not rejoice at wrongdoing, but rejoices with the truth. Love bears all things, believes all

things, hopes all things, endures all things. Love never ends.
[1 Corinthians 13:4-8]

Paul knew that God had particular reasons for ordaining the circumstances by which these people complicated his life work. He also knew the Old Testament Scriptures—for example, the longest psalm—which includes these words:

> Before I was afflicted I went astray, but now I keep your word. You are good and do good; teach me your statutes … It is good for me that I was afflicted, that I might learn your statutes … I know, O LORD, that your rules are righteous, and that in faithfulness you have afflicted me.
> [Psalm 119:67,68,71,75]

Here, an unnamed person of faith declared that it was good for him to have been afflicted, believing that his afflictions came from God. God *is* good, he wrote, and, in his faithfulness, God *does* what is good. Paul similarly knew, both from Scripture and personal experience, that some of the "good" afflictions that came to *him* from God were personally delivered through the misbehaviour of God's troublesome, disrespectful, and insulting people. Through them, God, *in his faithfulness*, taught Paul what this psalmist had been taught many centuries before about how to understand, and obey, the specific laws of God. So not only—not even primarily—because of the affection Paul had for the Corinthians, but because he was "under authority," he applied himself to the sometimes demanding, and even exasperating, duty of love.

In the same vein, Jesus instructed his apostles with these intriguing words:

> "Whoever has my commandments and keeps them, he it is who loves me. And <u>he who loves</u>

<u>me will be loved by my Father</u>, and I will love him …"
[John 14:21]

Are the followers of Christ *not* loved by the Father, and by Jesus, *until* they "have" his commandments and "keep" them? Obviously, this is a statement that warrants our careful attention, but it also sets us up to consider the second answer to that PRACTICAL QUESTION we looked at in Chapter 2; the question of what we can do to know Christ better, so as to be strengthened sufficiently to face the various challenges of living.

As our QUESTION's first answer lines up with Paul's first question of his Damascus Road introduction to Jesus, our second answer corresponds to Saul's second question, as we read it in Acts 22: the question of what his new Lord wanted him to do. Essentially, the very same question was asked again, a day or two later, by a disciple of Christ named Ananias. The book of Acts informs us that the Lord had spoken to him in a vision, calling him by name. Ananias replied, "Here I am, Lord" [Acts 9:10]. By this response, Ananias implied that he was willing and ready to do whatever the Lord commanded. And what *did* the Lord want him to do? Something very specific:

> Rise and go to the street called Straight, and at the house of Judas look for a man of Tarsus named Saul, for behold, he is praying, and he has seen in a vision a man named Ananias come in and lay his hands on him so that he might regain his sight.
> [Acts 9:11,12]

"A man of Tarsus named Saul"! Ananias had heard of the man—and he knew exactly *why* this "man of Tarsus" was in the city! "Lord, I have heard from many about this man, how much evil he has done to your saints at Jerusalem. And here he has authority from the chief priests to bind all who call on your name"

[Acts 9:13,14]. If Ananias seems disinclined to obey God, it is easy to understand why. (How inclined to obedience might Dietrich Bonhoeffer have been if God had instructed him, in 1944, to travel to Berlin in order to help a man named Hitler recover from a sudden case of blindness?) The Lord was insistent. "Go, for he is a chosen instrument of mine to carry my name before the Gentiles and kings and the children of Israel. For I will show him how much he must suffer for the sake of my name" [Acts 9:15,16]. So Ananias was told to go, and—being a Christian; a "man under authority"—he went:

> So Ananias departed and entered the house. And laying his hands on him he said, "Brother Saul, the Lord Jesus who appeared to you on the road by which you came has sent me so that you may regain your sight and be filled with the Holy Spirit." And immediately something like scales fell from his eyes, and he regained his sight.
> [Acts 9:17,18]

What Ananias had implied by saying, "Here I am, Lord," Saul's second question to Jesus stated plainly: "What shall I do?" [Acts 22:10]. And what were the Lord's instructions to Saul? To enter the city of Damascus, and to wait there for further instructions [Acts 22:10].

So it came about that Saul of Tarsus, the notorious enemy of what was initially known as "the Way" [Acts 9:2;19:23], regained his sight and was filled with the Holy Spirit—by the courageous help of a Christian who was simply following orders [Acts 9:11,12,17]. Then and there, Saul "was baptized, and taking food, he was strengthened. For some days he was with the disciples at Damascus." And, remarkably enough, "immediately he proclaimed Jesus in the synagogues, saying, 'He is the Son of God.'" Increasing "all the more in strength," Saul began to confound the Jews who lived in Damascus "by proving that Jesus was the Christ" [Acts 9:18-22]. In other words, in answer to Saul's question, what the Lord wanted Saul to do was to embark on a lifelong career of communicating the gospel, and defending the faith; or as we might say, a ministry of evangelism and apologetics. And, of course, church-planting! As this most unlikely new Christian remained faithful to his assignment, he was shown, as Ananias had been told he would be, "how much he must suffer for the sake of [Jesus'] name" [Acts 9:16].

But this suffering was not all that Saul was to be shown. He was also to be shown Jesus—and in a very remarkable way! The original 12 apostles, except for Judas Iscariot [John 13:21-30], were the first to hear of this new way of knowing Jesus. The very night he was betrayed by Judas, denied by Peter, and deserted by the other apostles, Jesus said:

> "Whoever has my commandments and keeps them, he it is who loves me. And he who loves me will be loved by my Father, and I will love him and manifest myself to him."
> [John 14:21]

There is, I think, a straightforward way to understand what Jesus was saying about *his* love, *and* the *love of the Father,* for his people. It is that, in the days that were soon to begin, a believer's deliberate obedience to Jesus, offered to God as a demonstration of love for Jesus, would have an outstanding result. The obedient follower of Jesus would be loved, both by God the Father, and by the Lord Jesus himself, to some previously unknown degree, or in some new manner. But what Jesus also was saying was that, in addition to that unprecedented demonstration of his love, he would also "manifest" himself to that particular obedient Christian. Curiously (I think), Jesus gave no details about this "manifestation"—not how it works or what it changes.

In the Face of People

By personal experience, what I have discovered in my intentional "commandment-keeping" (which, admittedly, has been more intentional at some times than at others), is that the difference this experience makes is like the difference between merely knowing *about* Jesus and actually, *relationally*, knowing him.

There is nothing to be said against knowing *about* Christ. Such knowledge is essential and foundational to any actual relationship with him. The nature of Christ's being, and his character, interests, and intentions, are learned through an accurate understanding of what the Bible reveals about him. We must not neglect to learn what the Scriptures reveal about the only human being in all of human history who is "the image of the invisible God" [Colossians 1:14], "the radiance of the glory of God and the exact imprint of his nature" [Hebrews 1:3]. If we fail to learn what the Bible declares *about* him, or if we wander away from what we have learned, we will almost certainly "re-image" him in our own likeness—or, worse, to our own liking. From there, we may continue to call ourselves worshippers of Christ, but we will have become idolaters. But knowing *about* Jesus is not the only sort of knowing. It is certainly not what Christ was speaking of when he said, in prayer, to his Father, "This is eternal life, that they know you the only true God, and Jesus Christ whom you have sent" [John 17:3]. The second answer then to our PRACTICAL QUESTION directs us to the experience of a *personal* knowledge of Christ. Again, the question is, **"What can we do to know Christ better and so be strengthened to face anything?"** And the second answer is, **"Identify the commandments of Christ and live in consistent obedience to them."**

Whatever troubles we encounter along the parade route—pain, change, "people problems," whatever!—Christ is with us, and able and willing to help us. Very often, I think, he helps us by strengthening our faith, and our hearts, so that we can get on with doing what he commands. Perhaps the trouble we are facing is the same as Paul encountered in loving those unlikable Corinthians. If so, we do not have to search for a relevant commandment of Christ to "keep." We already "have" one: to love even an unlikable believer with the sacrificial sort of love shown to us by Christ: the sort of love we feel might be the death of us, or, at least, the death of some part of us. Whatever specifically makes difficult such an act of obedience, Jesus knows exactly what we lack. Accordingly, he provides us with the precise sort of grace we require.

Perhaps it is patience we lack. Perhaps it is meekness, or wisdom, or courage. It makes no difference to Jesus what we are lacking. All of his grace is available to his people—all of the time. We do not need to deserve it. It is, after all, grace: the undeserved favour of God that he shows to those who actually deserve his disfavour! Every specific bit of help we need *is* ours for the asking—and available in abundance. It is in *this* regard that Paul wrote, "I can do all things through Christ who strengthens me" [Philippians 4:13]. And here is how the "manifesting" of Jesus begins.

As we trust Christ to help us "keep" his commandments, and as we prove that we trust him by taking corresponding steps of obedience, Jesus himself strengthens us for the task. In doing so, he introduces us to—or perhaps reacquaints us with—a particular aspect of his character. This *is* Christ manifesting himself.

To be perfectly clear on this, let us imagine a very specific example: the Lord's commandment about "foot-washing." The night he was betrayed, Jesus shocked his apostles by a particular example of the sort of love by which he expected them, as his disciples, to be known. To the apostles' surprise—and even disgust—it was slaves' work! The entire event is narrated in John 13:1-16. In the days of the apostles, household slaves were required to wash the dirty, and no doubt smelly, feet of the free members of the household, and of the guests who were invited to dinner. No one in those days, other than slaves, would even imagine stooping to such a depth of humiliation. But Jesus explained to them that it was what they "ought to do" [John 13:14,15]. The apostles should not have been shocked, for he had previously said to them, "Whoever would be great among you must be your servant, and whoever would be first among you must be slave of all" [Mark 10:43,44].

With this "foot-washing" event as an example, the commandment of Jesus is to take on the role of a slave in order to meet the needs of our brothers and sisters. That would include, of course, the needs of a person we find ourselves not liking. Just imagine! Perhaps, an unexpected phone call reveals that the appropriate application of this commandment is to drive across town and sit by the sickbed of an awkward and unlikable church acquaintance who is evidently afflicted with a bad case of the flu. As you might have expected, that evening, that which you feared the most comes upon you. It turns out you are the only person in the room—in fact, the house—when the sudden consequences of a violent attack of nausea make themselves visible. As a slave of Christ, you are under orders! Fetching a bucket of hot soapy water and several rags simply to hand to the pathetic wretch in the bed would *not* be a good and faithful slave's response. Jesus is calling you to do the work yourself! And the "manifesting" of Jesus will begin as you do. He himself will strengthen you to do it, with whatever strength you require. The strength of back and legs to kneel; the strength of arms and hands to scrub; perhaps the strength of stomach to get through the ordeal without creating more of a similar mess. Most to the point, you can count on your master to provide you with the self-control, the humility, and the love of Christ required to get the whole mess cleaned up with an attitude of a good and faithful slave. You will know you are meeting the standard when you hear yourself assuring the person, convincingly, that you count the entire experience a privilege, because of what Jesus said about "foot-washing." And you will know more *experientially* of the character of Christ, who "came not to be served but to serve, and to give his life as a ransom for many" [Mark 10:45]. In your act of obedience, Christ was "manifesting" himself, that is, making himself known to you.

As we receive from Christ his strength, we experientially grow in our knowledge of him: not in "head knowledge" (although without *that* kind of knowledge, we wouldn't know what he meant by such phrases as "foot-washing"), but in "suds-in-the-bucket, knees-on-the-floor, character-building, relationship-changing knowledge": the knowledge that strengthens us to be recognized as his disciples. Our experience will be just as Jesus said:

> "A new commandment I give to you, that you love one another: just as I have loved you, you also are to love one another. By this all people will know that you are my disciples, if you have love for one another."
> [John 13:34, 35]

The difference that this new experiential element will make to our relationship with Jesus should overwhelm us with anticipation. This difference can be compared to progressing from regularly and happily doing research on some famous person you are interested in—which is what Answer #1 is all about—to picking up the phone and calling that celebrity; especially if he or she picks up, and the phone call turns out to go so well that you and he or she develop a regular routine of phoning each other. Especially if, in time, you become the best of friends. And maybe, as you two get better acquainted, you discover that your new best friend is the kindest and wisest person you have ever met: always interested in what is new with you, and always full of good and really helpful advice. Imagine it!

Additionally, being a very generous person—a billionaire several times over, of course—your new best friend is only too happy to ship to you anything you ever might happen to need, and many of the things you would simply just enjoy. "Oh no," says the celebrity again and again. "It is my great pleasure to prove to you how much

I just really like you. Never hesitate to ask for things, my friend. Now what size of a sailboat are you thinking would be nicest? Or would you rather have a summer cottage?"

As a daydream with a purpose, it might actually benefit you to select an actual person, both rich and famous: a film star, a member of the royal family, or a professional athlete, and imagine this "biographical-research-turned-permanent-friendship" experience. But just for a few minutes! Having imagined it, you can then deliberately settle yourself down to think again about what Jesus explained so plainly in John 14:21.

Dr. John Owen, the brilliant 17th century pastor, theologian and author, would not have thought of Paul's "people problems" in Corinth as incidental, insignificant or unimportant. In 1673, at the age of 57, Dr. Owen preached a sermon entitled "*Gospel Charity*" [or as we would say it: "Gospel Love"]. The sermon explained that the integrity and intensity of the love we Christians have *for one another* indicates the genuineness of our faith in Christ.

To that point, Owen made this blunt but helpful statement: "Let none, then, pretend that they love the brethren in general, and love the people of God, and love the saints, while their love is not fervently exercised towards those who are in the same church society with them. Christ hath given it you for a trial." By "a trial," Owen means a test. In other words, God has brought the members of your own church family into *your* life to test the authenticity of your faith.

"Faith is trusting God enough to obey him," I often used to say to the West London church family. It was the short version of my own formal definition of faith as "the desire and the ability to trust and obey God"—obeying him, for example, when he commands us to love our "neighbor," to love one another, and to love our enemies.

The New Testament letter we know as 1st Peter promises its readers that, "after they have suffered a little while," God by his grace will himself "restore, confirm, strengthen, and establish" them [1 Peter 5:10]. And who were these people who were receiving such a promise? People who the Apostle Peter called "elect exiles" [1 Peter 1:1], that is, people chosen by God and living as "outsiders" in this world: women and men, youth and children, who, having come to Christ through faith, are now "like living stones … being built up as a spiritual house and a holy priesthood to offer spiritual sacrifices acceptable to God through Jesus Christ" [1 Peter 2:5].

The Apostle Paul used this same "temple metaphor" to describe the connection of each Christian to each other, and to Christ [Ephesians 2:19-22]. But he also taught that Christians should think of themselves as the various "members" (by which he meant, "body parts") of an actual human body, with Christ himself being the "head" of that "body" [1 Corinthians 12:12-27; Ephesians 4:11-16].

Now here's the thing. *Being* the actual people who God will "restore, confirm, strengthen, and establish," and *being* a "living stone" of the sort that "the temple of God" is constructed, are *not* experiences unrelated to each other. God's intention to "restore, confirm, strengthen, and establish" his people has *everything* to do with his people being living pieces of a particular "temple" in which God is worshipped. None of it happens to people who never *actually* attach themselves to each other in some actual church.

The alarming alternative for every believer is to be like a stone that has miraculously been brought to life, but just lies in a field (or in a parking lot—even a church parking lot!); breathing and feeling and thinking, but not accomplishing what God brought it to life for the purpose of accomplishing.

Alternately, believing in Christ but not belonging to one of his churches is like being a human body part (say, a kidney), lying on a stainless steel shelf in an Operating Room, all set to be transplanted into a human body (that could really use another good kidney about now), but that never actually gets attached, in the right way, to a human body at all. As all real churches need real Christians in order to be what God by his grace has created churches to be, so every actual Christian needs to belong to an actual church in order to be what God by his grace has re-created him or her to become. So isn't it surprising that there seems to be so many people who love God and serve Jesus but never get around to becoming an active member of a church, and so many Christians who have "given up" on the "organized church"?

As a long-time actual pastor, I know that often the explanation is that, the self-identified Lone Christian has given a church—or two or three—a try, and was hurt. That is always a sad story. But on the testimony of three witnesses (Peter and Paul, the apostles, and John Owen, the pastor), no one said being a "living stone" in a "temple" made of people, or a living "member" in a human body whose "head" is Christ, would be nothing but helium balloons and sparklers. When the Apostle Peter spoke of "suffering for a little while," he may not have meant only the suffering of great persecution, torture and dungeon time, or, in our day, and this part of the world, being ridiculed or ostracized or professionally excluded from promotions and privileges. Peter might also have been thinking of the many little sufferings involved in deliberately loving the annoying and perhaps demanding—even exasperating—people who you get to know when you commit yourself to serving Christ in one of his churches.

Paul had this same understanding of his obligation to love the people (all the people!) of the church in Corinth. His letter reveals he was quite clear about *why* some of them were a part of his life; and of how God was using the difficult ones to conform him more fully to the image of Christ. In contrast, it seems that, all the while Job suffered, and even for the subsequent years he lived after being restored to his previous "blessed" state, he never did learn a thing about why God ordained the details of his life, for a time, to be so "full of trouble" [Job 14:1].

The Old Testament also tells the story of a man with devastating "people problems, who unlike Job, did eventually learn the reasons—at least one big reason—why God had orchestrated his "trouble." The man was Joseph, and he was problematically well-known to be the favourite son of his father, Jacob. In due time, predictably enough, Joseph became the target of his ten jealous brothers' contempt. He was just 17 years old.[9]

It was decades later that Joseph discovered one very good thing that God was accomplishing by the evil brought upon him by his brothers. About 22 years after they had sold him to slave traders, who "just happened" to be on a business trip to Egypt, Joseph's older brothers found themselves standing very nervously before him. But now he was adorned in Egyptian splendour. They didn't recognize him, but since they had last seen him, Joseph had somehow become a powerful official in the courts of the Pharaoh. And there they were, having travelled a great distance to beg the king of Egypt for the bread that was needed to survive a major famine. Now imagine the brothers' thinking, and terror, as they heard what Joseph had to say:

> "I am your brother, Joseph, whom you sold into Egypt. And now do not be distressed or angry with yourselves because you sold me here, for <u>God sent me</u> before you to preserve life … <u>God sent me</u> before you to preserve for you a remnant on earth, and to keep alive for you many survivors. So <u>it was not you who sent me here, but God</u>."
> [Genesis 45:4-8]

---

9   The entire story of Joseph is told in Chapters 37-50 of the book of Genesis.

In the Face of People

Sometime later, the plot thickened considerably for Joseph's brothers. Their father Jacob died, an event which seemed to spell trouble to them:

> When Joseph's brothers saw that their father was dead, they said, "It may be that Joseph will hate us and pay us back for all the evil that we did to him." So they sent a message to Joseph, saying, "Your father gave this command before he died: 'Say to Joseph, "Please forgive the transgression of your brothers and their sin, because they did evil to you."' And now, please forgive the transgression of the servants of the God of your father."
>
> Joseph wept when they spoke to him. His brothers also came and fell down before him and said, "Behold, we are your servants." But Joseph said to them, "Do not fear, for am I in the place of God? As for you, <u>you meant evil against me, but God meant it for good</u>, to bring it about that many people should be kept alive, as they are today. So do not fear; I will provide for you and your little ones." Thus he comforted them and spoke kindly to them.
> [Genesis 50:15-21]

The long story concludes with Joseph stating what God "meant" by the suffering brought upon him by his brothers' cruelty. Although Joseph was legally empowered to mistreat them, as they certainly deserved, he graciously provided them and their families with the grain they needed to survive the famine.

So, Joseph eventually became clear on why such terrible things had happened to him. But for his many years of suffering—from the age of 17 until he was turning 40—his only hope for the future came from what he knew about the God of his fathers. In answer to the obvious and painful question of why such "evil" had happened to him, he could only wait to discover, in God's time, what "good and acceptable and perfect" thing God "meant" by it all. Twenty years is a long time for a teenager to wait for such an explanation. But many *centuries* were to pass before Joseph's life story began to be seen for what else it was: a foreshadowing of the character and life work of Christ.

During the years that Jesus lived in Galilee, and repeatedly travelled back and forth to Judea, he miraculously fed a large crowd of hungry people. In fact, he performed this miracle twice [Matthew 16:9,10]. Immediately after one of these displays of his power and benevolence, Jesus made a great claim—an impossibly audacious claim if it were not true:

> "I am the bread of life; whoever comes to me shall not hunger, and whoever believes in me shall never thirst. But I said to you that you have seen me and yet do not believe."
> [John 6:35]

The book of Genesis reveals that, many centuries before this spectacular claim, Joseph, an ancestor of Jesus, had lived out a sort of preview of him and his life work. Joseph gave his brothers the bread by which they survived, although they did not deserve such kindness. In a way that resembled the future claim, and the actual work, of the living "bread of life," Joseph graciously saved his entire family.

Additionally, Joseph's troubles set him up to demonstrate practically the love that Christ commands *us* to show one another: that gracious and generous love of God that we are commanded to demonstrate even to complicated "problem people." It is easy enough for us to see that God uses all sorts of people (Joseph and Paul, for example), to inspire and direct us as slaves of Christ.

In the Face of People

Less noticeable, perhaps, is the important and practical truth that, as God used Joseph's hateful brothers in his life, and as God used complicated Corinthians in Paul's, so God uses our "problem people" to accomplish his work in us, especially the good of us being conformed to the image of Christ [Romans 8:28,29].

So let us agree, O good and faithful slaves of Jesus—in direct obedience to his commandments, and in demonstration of our love for him—to get on with the assignment. Let us boldly step forward to sacrificially love and serve people, even if we do not like them at all. Let us love them authentically, deliberately, and actively. As we do, we will learn, from the adventures into which our love leads us, how able and willing Christ is to strengthen us in our obedience to him. And we will discover for ourselves the practical implications of what Jesus once said about his "yoke" and his "burden":

> "Come to me, all who labor and are heavy laden, and I will give you rest. Take my yoke upon you, and learn from me, for I am gentle and lowly in heart, and you will find rest for your souls. For my yoke is easy, and my burden is light."
> [Matthew 11:28-30]

Both in the Old Testament and the New, a yoke is a symbol of slavery [e.g. Leviticus 26:13; Galatians 5:1]. Christ's "yoke" represents our duties as his slaves. His "burden" is the workload we bear as we serve him. Speaking to "heavy laden" people, Jesus explained that, in comparison to working for any other master, serving him is "easy." And the assignments he places on our agendas are relatively "light." What keeps our slavery from exhausting us, of course, is that he himself provides us with the specific strength our obedience requires. Serving a master as "gentle and lowly in heart" as Jesus, we will find that, even in the heaviest parts of our work, he generously provides us with "rest for our souls."

Christianity's critics have often taken a negative view of serving Christ, as if they knew more about serving Christ than do his faithful servants. But G.K. Chesterton explained, "The Christian ideal has not been tried and found wanting. It has been found difficult; and left untried."

As servants aspiring to be good and faithful, let us then get on with doing "all we are commanded" [Luke 17:10]. Our good, kind, and generous master has given us strict orders about loving people. Let us not leave any one of his commandments "untried." And let us look forward, with hearts full of wonder, to the unique and glory-filled "*John-Fourteen-Twenty-Wonderfulness*" of it all.

A PRACTICAL QUESTION:

What can we do to know Christ better and so be strengthened to face anything?

"*Who are you, Lord?*"

1. Learn as much about Christ as we can from diligent reading and study of the Bible. (John 5:39)

"*What shall I do, Lord?*"

2. Identify the commandments of Christ and live in consistent obedience to them. (John 14:21)

Chapter 5.   THE FACE IN THE MIRROR

> in which we face our most personal "people problem"
>
> *Who is sufficient for these things? ... Such is the confidence that we have through Christ toward God ... our sufficiency is from God, who has made us sufficient...*
> [2 Corinthians 2:16-3:6]

One of the pleasures of my current circumstances is the now-not-unusual experience of being contacted by, and then having lunch or a coffee with, someone who, for some time in the past, was a part of the church I pastored. Happily (so far), not one of them has taken this initiative in order to articulate some offense or displeasure with my ministry, although I *am* quite able to list a number of people—to myself, so don't ask me—whose motivation for such a meeting would be of that sort. So far, the people calling the meetings have been appreciative and kind, and these get-togethers have been pleasant, and often amusing.

Regularly, the conversation turns to something I apparently once said, in a sermon, or a Bible study, or privately. Frequently, I have no recollection of ever saying what I am then quoted on. Here is a recent example:

> HIM: *"I have always remembered your Two Keys of Perseverance."*
> ME: *"Two keys? Remind me."*
> HIM: *"To know what you are competent at. And to keep showing up."*

I do remember feeling competent. Because of the mentoring I had received from the pastor I worked for in Toronto, I began my London ministry with some sense that I *was* actually good at some aspects of the work. There were, of course, other parts of pastoral ministry for which I felt barely adequate, and still other parts I had yet to experience. Down at that end of the wading pool, "competent" is what I did *not* feel.

But I did move to London with confidence. Having followed around my pastor-turned-boss-turned-mentor for over three years, watching and listening to him in pastoral action, and having a weekly food-court lunch with him to tell him what I had said and done that week, and hearing him explain what I *should* have said and done, I was fairly sure that, as the need arose, I would probably be able to pull off a reasonable impersonation of him.

As it turned out, there were occasions in those early years when I did find myself "just fakin' it," to quote a Jewish man named Paul who was *not* an apostle. My first memorable moments of fakery took place at the first funeral I officiated. That was the day I learned, very suddenly, that the minister conducting the funeral rides from the chapel to the cemetery in the procession's lead car. I was walking out of the chapel with the family of the deceased, immediately after the service, when I noticed the funeral director holding open the passenger door of the front limousine. He was looking at me, and it seemed that he expected me to be his passenger. Risking all, I walked confidently toward him, nodded, and got into the car, and without comment, he quietly closed the door. As he walked around the front of the vehicle to take his place behind the wheel, I quietly sighed in relief, reflecting on what would have happened if I had guessed wrongly about who rides with him. Some small talk ensued, and I did my best to participate in a voice that sounded pastorally experienced. But halfway to our destination, the director turned to me and asked, "Will you be using sand, Reverend?"

"Sand?" I asked myself. I had no idea what he meant. Hoping for the best, I suavely replied, "Well, no. I have never used sand." And I spent the rest of that weekend wondering what some officiating ministers *do* use sand for.

As the years of my London pastorate continued, becoming, for the most part, more and more pleasant to me, (and, apparently, sufficiently pleasant to a majority of the elders), I began to observe that some of my pastoral colleagues, serving in other churches, and in other denominations, were not finding much pleasure in their work. In fact, some of my acquaintances were finding their work stressful—even unmanageably so. It seemed to me that, in some cases, the problem was nothing more complicated than a lack of the necessary skills required to shepherd a church; skills such as weekly sermon-writing, confident public speaking, effective problem-solving, reasonable goal-setting, inspiring vision-casting, and non-stupid decision-making. I noticed that while some of these beleaguered young pastors stepped down from their positions— and not always voluntarily—others bravely remained at the helm, continuing to endure the storms of "the difficult and unrewarding life" of a pastor.

To refuse to surrender under enemy fire can seem to be the right thing to do. To choose to endure the "outrageous fortune" of church leadership can seem a noble course. But at times it appeared to me that some of the "slings and arrows" hitting their mark were signs that the leadership role was simply "not a good fit." My hunches were reinforced by my memories of student days. Some of my teachers and professors clearly loved their work, and were obviously loved and appreciated by their students: me, for example. But other teachers seemed uncomfortable in the classroom, or at the front of the lecture hall. Some were just not good teachers. I concluded that the work of a pastor, like the work of a teacher, was not for everyone.

I could not stop myself from comparing these sad stories to my own pastoral experience. (Perhaps I *could* have—and *should* have—but I didn't.) These comparisons settled a conviction in my mind that I was, to an adequate degree, competent. I made no claim to be a great pastor, or an exceptionally gifted one. But I did feel "up to the task," and believed that the explanation was that pastoring a church is what God had designed me, and then called me, to do.

And then years of church life happened, with many pastoral adventures; some of them of a distinctly humiliating sort. I did make some rookie mistakes, and some stupid decisions. I launched some questionable initiatives; improperly responded to some intentional aggravation, and sometimes gave biblically-sound but clumsily-worded advice. And one Sunday morning after the Service, I lost my temper and used a mild profanity to tell off a grumpy old man. (The widow of one of my pastoral predecessors was standing next to him at the time.)

Such non-fatal disasters, and their accompanying bouts of well-deserved mental anguish and frustration, did not prove to be the ruin of my ministry. Rather, the experiences served me as sea anchors, slowing me down, and steadying me, through a variety of hard but survivable pastoral squalls. So it turned out, that, by the grace of God, and by the "sufficiency" that he freely provided [Romans 8:32], I never did smash the good ship "West London" on a deadly reef, and the crew never made me "walk the plank."

What else happened was that I tried to make sense of the opposite sort of pastoral experience. Quite regularly, kind-hearted people would describe to me, or to others in my hearing, that some pastoral thing I had done was "just really excellent." A sermon I had preached. Pastoral counsel I had given. An act of leadership I had demonstrated. A wedding or a funeral I had officiated. Even a common act of courtesy that was noticed and considered too lowly a deed for the pastor to stoop to. People often said, "You are an excellent pastor, Pastor Mike!" And I was left to figure out what to make of such accolades.

What I worked out was that these appreciative and encouraging people were noticing, and generously commenting on, nothing more than pastoral competence—as well as the good manners I learned from my mother, and the gentlemen's courtesy I learned from my father. It did seem to me that these compliments were sometimes so lofty only because competence was so uncommon. What I then began to tell myself—and occasionally passed on to others—was that "competence looks like excellence in the midst of mediocrity." I realized then, and still do, that the statement sounds smug: "self-righteously and annoyingly complacent," as any good thesaurus might put it. Admittedly, it also sounds cynical, and worse yet, an unkind thing to say in reference to certain unnamed colleagues of mine. For this reason, I passed it on only occasionally. But the statement helped *me*, at least, to avoid taking too seriously the extreme accolades that sometimes came, and still come, my way, about being "an excellent pastor." And it helped me make a private deal with myself. I would give the high-rolling compliments no more weight than I give the creative and imaginative criticisms that, especially in the early years, came my way. I formed a mental image of all the personal comments as a loaf of bread; a long loaf from which I would slice off, and throw away, both "heels." My middle-of-the-loaf conclusions on the whole matter were two: that pastoral work demands competence; and that, by God's great grace, I had some.

By the time I moved to London, I had learned to look to God for strength and confidence, for I was powerfully influenced by my understanding of what the Apostle Paul wrote to the Corinthians about "competence" as a gift of God. The English Standard Version of the Bible (which I am happily using) translates as "sufficiency" the Greek word that, in other verses, and other versions, is rendered "competence" and "adequacy." For example, Paul wrote, "Our sufficiency [or, competence, or adequacy] is from God, who has made us sufficient [or, competent, or adequate] to be ministers of a new covenant …" [2 Corinthians 3:5,6].

"Competence is a gift of God, Wilkins," I was able to tell myself, as I took up the many responsibilities of my new life—"fakin' it" sometimes, and trying at all times to remember to trust God. Since I had reasons to believe that my opportunity to pastor the church had been God's idea in the first place, I knew I would find his grace more than enough for the challenges of each day. At the same time, I was learning to look to God for the "sufficiency" to be a good husband and father, since he had given me those privileges and responsibilities, too.

So I kept showing up at church on Sundays, and on many of the days in-between, trusting God to provide me with an appropriate amount of competence for every occasion. And after Sunday morning services, and at the end of each workday, I kept showing up at home, trying to enter the house remembering that, along with the confusion of kids' shoes and toys and books that might be piled up against the doors of the front hall closet, there would always also be a pile of God's grace waiting there for me. With this important truth in mind, I worked on preventing my children from the disturbing sight of their father—the church's smiling, warm-hearted pastor—morphing into their family's grumpy, hot-tempered Dad as he entered the house.

We have seen that Paul's relationship to the Christians in Corinth was complicated. To a great degree, the relational challenges that

The Face in the Mirror

Paul experienced, and addressed, were fueled by the church's doubts about the legitimacy of his apostleship. Inadvertently, Paul himself might have intensified this blazing church fire by writing in his previous letter: "I am the least of the apostles, unworthy to be called an apostle, because I persecuted the church of God" [1 Corinthians 15:9]. "Told ya," one unhappy church member might have said to another. What Paul's doubters and critics should have understood as his genuine humility, they took as evidence of his "inadequacy." What they should have recognized as a God-glorifying declaration of his own inherent unworthiness, they interpreted as his lack of the competence required to exercise authority over them [1 Peter 5:2].

Responding boldly, Paul challenged their low view of him and his role in their lives:

> Who is sufficient for these things? For we are not, like so many, peddlers of God's word, but as men of sincerity, as commissioned by God, in the sight of God we speak in Christ. Are we beginning to commend ourselves again? Or do we need, as some do, letters of recommendation to you, or from you?
> [2 Corinthians 2:16-3:1]

Letters of recommendation? Under the circumstances, letters of that sort might have been just the thing! Letters of approval from the Apostles Peter, James and John? The whole matter of legitimacy might have been thoroughly, and promptly, settled! Quite probably, such letters would have been easy for Paul to arrange [Acts 15:22-26]. But he had another idea. His response to the lack of respect was to explain that, actually, he *did* have a letter—and these Corinthian church members were it!

> You yourselves are our letter of recommendation, written on our hearts, to be known and read by

all. And you show that you are a letter from Christ delivered by us, written not with ink but with the Spirit of the living God, not on tablets of stone but on tablets of human hearts. Such is the confidence that we have through Christ toward God. [2 Corinthians 3:2-4]

Speaking on his own behalf, but also on Timothy's, Paul was essentially saying:

> "If it is a letter you wish to see, look at our hearts. A letter of recommendation is there for anyone to read. And anyone who takes the time to understand our motives—our love for you, and our commitment to the enriching of your relationship to God—will see from whom this letter comes. It comes from Jesus Christ! He himself dictated it to the Holy Spirit. The Spirit of the living God has written you Corinthian Christians on our hearts."

Paul and Timothy's love for these annoyingly insubordinate Christians, and the "patience, kindness, goodness, faithfulness, gentleness, and self-control" with which Paul and Timothy interacted with them, was visible and tangible proof of the legitimacy of their ministry. By the power of Christ's Spirit, these two men were bearing "the fruit of the Spirit" [Galatians 5:22,23], like branches abiding on a vine, as Jesus explained:

> "I am the true vine, and my Father is the vinedresser ... Abide in me, and I in you. As the branch cannot bear fruit by itself, unless it abides in the vine, neither can you, unless you abide in me. I am the vine; you are the branches. Whoever abides in

me and I in him, he it is that bears much fruit, for apart from me you can do nothing."
[John 15:1-5]

God, like a vine-dresser, was using both men to bear that same fruit in the church in Corinth. Thus Paul and Timothy proved that they *were* authentic disciples of Christ. And God was pleased. As Christ himself had said it: "By this my Father is glorified, that you bear much fruit and so prove to be my disciples" [John 15:8].

As for the question of competence, Paul's confidence was "through Christ" and "toward God," from whom he and Timothy were made "sufficient to be ministers." It was God, through Christ, who had performed the transformation of Saul. Once an angry "blasphemer, persecutor, and insolent opponent" of the gospel, Paul had been transformed into a Spirit-empowered "preacher and apostle and teacher." Paul could be confident that Christ would always supply him with strength, and richly provide him with whatever was required to take on every challenge involved in the work of the gospel—and so can we!

This work of the gospel can be seen as two parts of a whole project. One half of the work is "getting the gospel—God's good news—out" to people of every nation, including our own. Specifically, this work is to communicate the good news about Jesus to people of every linguistic, cultural and ethnic background, seeking to persuade them to entrust themselves to Christ, if God would be pleased to make it happen. Through the power of the gospel, these people commit their lives to "his kingdom … and his righteousness" [Matthew 6:33]. In other words, "getting the gospel *out*" is communicating to people the "news" that Christ's work on the earth—especially his work on the cross—provides forgiveness of sins, and the gift of eternal life, to everyone who truly believes in Jesus. This work is often called evangelism.

Glory in the Face

At West London, for years, the other half of the work of the gospel has been known as "getting the gospel *in*." What we mean is the work of getting God's good news into the interior of the life of people who *do* believe in Jesus. These people are already "Christians," in the biblical sense of the Word [Acts 11:26]. But they still need their minds more thoroughly renewed and their lives more thoroughly transformed [Romans 12:1,2]. This second half of the work of the gospel is, in itself, a sort of "missionary work." But here the "mission field" is the inner life of one particular Christian, rather than the native land of any particular people. As on other mission fields, this assignment eventually reaches a frontier. There, the joyful message must be carried across some sort of border into some sort of dark place, to which the news has never been carried: an "unreached" corner of that Christian's inner life. There, the light of the gospel must shine, so that the darkness might be destroyed. Then, a certain aspect of life will be liberated instead of enslaved, or at least enfeebled, by enemies of the soul. So one follower of Christ labours to strengthen the spiritual life of another follower of Christ. This work is commonly called "discipleship."

Of course, God is perfectly able on his own to accomplish both halves of this work. But as it is with many compassionate parents, God the Father delights to arrange things in such a way that his children work alongside him:

> All this is from God, who through Christ reconciled us to himself and gave us the ministry of reconciliation; that is, in Christ God was reconciling the world to himself, not counting their trespasses against them, and entrusting to us the message of reconciliation. Therefore, <u>we are ambassadors for Christ, God making his appeal through us</u>. We implore you on behalf of Christ, be reconciled to God. For our sake he made him to be sin who

knew no sin, so that in him we might become the righteousness of God. <u>Working together with him</u>, then, we appeal to you not to receive the grace of God in vain.
[2 Corinthians 5:18-6:1]

As we look more closely at this honour of "working together" with God, we can see that this second half of the work ("getting the gospel in") also has two parts. Alongside the mission of "discipling" Christians, still young in the faith (or perhaps not young, but stuck, and therefore no longer progressing), is the gospel worker's additional assignment of "getting the gospel in" to the frontiers of his or her *own* inner life. So it is with all partners in the work of the gospel of God [Philippians 1:3-5]. Every person who has been "washed and sanctified and justified in the name of the Lord Jesus Christ and by the Spirit of God" [1 Corinthians 6:11] has the continuing obligation—and the need—"to grow in the grace and knowledge of the Lord Jesus Christ" [2 Peter 3:18].

And there is still one more division of the work into two parts! "Getting the gospel in" to your own private life requires both "yard work" and "house work." The "yard work" calls for improving and intensifying our outward obedience to God, and our visible and audible imitation of Christ, in our spoken words and actions. Regarding this part of the assignment, Paul again is an excellent role model. Previously, he had written to the Corinthians:

> Do you not know that in a race all the runners run, but only one receives the prize? So run that you may obtain it. Every athlete exercises self-control in all things. They do it to receive a perishable wreath, but we an imperishable. So I do not run aimlessly; I do not box as one beating the air. But I discipline my body and keep it under

control, lest after preaching to others I myself should be disqualified.
[1 Corinthians 9:24-27]

With these words, Paul explained that, in regard to *this* specific assignment, our efforts must rise to the standards of a serious athlete who "exercises self-control in all things." Our appetites, our conflicting intentions, our natural ways of wasting time, must all be brought under control. We have been called to assume the determination of a competitive runner who fully intends to win the race, or a boxer who is determined to be the one standing when the bell rings. We are required to "discipline" our bodies, keeping them "under control." At this level of competition, the stakes are very high. In Paul's day, the winner's "prize" was a wreath; a meaningful but perishable award. At stake for us is "an imperishable wreath:" a reward that is long-lasting—in fact, everlasting. The alternative to "winning," Paul warns, is the alarming spiritual equivalent of being "disqualified" from the competition![10]

As crucial as this "yard work" is, even *more* important is the "housework." For, in the case of every human life, the mess in the yard is always related to the clutter indoors. All that we say and do—all of our spoken, written (and texted and "tweeted"!) words—and all of our actions, commendable or otherwise, can be traced to the state of our minds and hearts. For this reason, Paul often addressed the essential need we all have to control our minds. His specific directives still raise powerful questions for anyone seeking to follow his example. As a case in point, as Paul was winding down his letter to the Philippians, he wrote, "Finally, brothers, whatever is true, whatever is honorable, whatever is just,

---

10 The warning becomes all the more alarming when these last verses of 1 Corinthians 9 are considered in connection to the statements that we know as the first thirteen verses of Chapter 10.

whatever is pure, whatever is lovely, whatever is commendable, if there is any excellence, if there is anything worthy of praise, think about these things" [Philippians 4:8]. The powerful question before us is: What *do* we think about when our minds are free to choose the topic? (Or as Peter Sarstedt sang in 1969, "Where do you go to, my lovely, when you're alone in your bed?")

As challenging as the control of the mind is, the heart presents a greater challenge, and a more critical one. The heart is even a greater influence upon us—and by our hearts we are defined. God himself informed the prophet Samuel, "The LORD sees not as man sees: man looks on the outward appearance, but the LORD looks on the heart" [1 Samuel 16:7]. In this plain Old Testament statement of fact, God revealed that what is of primary importance to him, in his appraisal of a person, is the heart. For in the heart are hidden our most fervent loves and our most intense hatreds.

Left to its own devices, the heart presents a very alarming picture. As Jesus explained, "Out of the heart come evil thoughts, murder, adultery, sexual immorality, theft, false witness, slander. These are what defile a person" [Matthew 15:19,20]. But our wisest, and most righteous, words and actions also come from our hearts. Our words and deeds, and even our thoughts—whether pure and praise-worthy, or polluted and poisonous—are formed by what we love and what we hate the most. But the thing is, neither our capacity to love or to hate is good or evil in itself. Loving *some* things is a great wickedness to God: violence, for example, and cruelty. *Hating* some things greatly pleases God; things such as pride and injustice. The management of both "heart conditions" requires wisdom and watchful attention. Accordingly, the Bible's collection of "wisdom principles" includes this frank warning: "Keep your heart with all vigilance, for from it flow the springs of life" [Proverbs 4:23].

Real wisdom requires a precise knowledge of what God himself loves and hates. For example: "he loves righteous deeds" [Psalm

11:7]. "He loves righteousness and justice" [Psalm 33:5]. "He loves him who pursues righteousness" [Proverbs 15:9]. "God loves a cheerful giver" [2 Corinthians 9:7]. On the other hand:

> There are six things that the LORD hates, seven that are an abomination to him: haughty eyes, a lying tongue, and hands that shed innocent blood, a heart that devises wicked plans, feet that make haste to run to evil, a false witness who breathes out lies, and one who sows discord among brothers.
> [Proverbs 6:16-19]

Only God—Father, Son and Holy Spirit—is perfectly righteous both in what he loves, and in what he hates. The Son of God, anointed by God as "the King of kings and Lord of lords" [Revelation 19:16], is praised by the Father specifically because of the Father's delight in his loves and hatreds; in other words, because of the condition of his heart. So the Father, addressing the Son as "God," praises him with these words:

> Your throne, O God, is forever and ever, the scepter of uprightness is the scepter of your kingdom. You have loved righteousness and hated wickedness; therefore God, your God, has anointed you with the oil of gladness beyond your companions.
> [Hebrews 1:8,9]

Here, quoting Psalm 45, the author of Hebrews makes it perfectly clear that, in the mind, and the heart, of God, the most notable and important thing about a human being, even the one unique and perfect human being, is the state of his heart, as revealed by his loves and his hatreds. So then, where does that leave us?

The Face in the Mirror

At times—and this is one—there's nothing like a good mirror for seeing yourself—or some part of yourself that you can't see on your own. But the particular mirror we need the most is the kind that allows us to see the condition of our own heart: the part of our inner life that God especially "looks upon." In the New Testament letter written by James, a figure of speech is used to introduce that particular sort of mirror:

> If anyone is a hearer of the word and not a doer, he is like a man who looks intently at his natural face in a mirror. For he looks at himself and goes away and at once forgets what he was like. But the one who looks into the perfect law, the law of liberty, and perseveres, being no hearer who forgets but a doer who acts, he will be blessed in his doing.
> [James 1:23,24]

A person who looks "intently" into a mirror, but then forgets what he or she saw, is missing out on one of the mirror's most practical uses. Picture a young boy playing with the small mirror he recently found in his mother's purse. On a bright and sunny summer morning, he finds all sorts of ways to have fun with it. Pretending to be stranded on a desert island, he uses the mirror to start a small sidewalk fire, and then to signal a helicopter flying overhead. Then, in the mood to annoy his sister, he positions the mirror to reflect sunshine into her eyes, as she plays with her friend across the street. But the boy fails to use the mirror to discover that some of the chocolate, which he also found in his mother's purse, is now quite noticeably smeared across his chin. And ... up the sidewalk comes his mother, just finishing her mid-morning run!

The Bible is precisely the mirror we need. The point James was making is that the Word of God, "the perfect law, the law of liberty," provides us with the self-awareness we need. The Word of God enables us, especially from its disclosure of God's moral expectations, to discern the condition of our own hearts. The Bible reveals to us the sorts of passions our heart should be filled with, and the unholy loves and unrighteous hatreds that have no legitimate place in our hearts.

Another biblical metaphor for the Word of God points to a similar usefulness:

> The word of God is living and active, sharper than any two-edged sword, piercing to the division of soul and of spirit, of joints and of marrow, and discerning the thoughts and intentions of the heart.
> [Hebrews 4:12]

"Discerning the thoughts and intentions of the heart." How useful and essential a tool! This sharp sword, uniquely capable of dividing and discerning what is actually going on within us, is the gift that God has given us in answer to that most personal and introspective prayer of the man after God's heart:

> Search me, O God, and know my heart!
> Try me and know my thoughts!
> And see if there be any grievous way in
> me, and lead me in the way everlasting!
> [Psalm 139:23,24]

On an unexpectedly-related note (no, really), in the closing minutes of my favourite movie (in the category of "Romantic Comedy with Endearing Metaphysical Moments"), Joe Banks asks Patricia Graynamore—at a very desperate moment for both of them—an important question that she is able to answer matter-of-factly:

HE: *So what are we hoping for?*
SHE: *A miracle.*
HE: *OK. A miracle.*[11]

Sometimes life is like that. Sometimes, what we really need *is* a miracle—a change that only God himself can bring about. Sometimes, only a miracle can fix what needs fixing. This is the position we come to once the first two answers to our PRACTICAL QUESTION have become *consistent* parts of our lives. As we have seen, what we gain from knowing *about* Christ through the diligent study of the Scriptures, and how we come to know Christ personally as he *manifests* himself to us, is foundational to the knowledge of Christ that our lives and our challenges require. But once both practices become settled parts of our lives, we see that what we *still* need is a miracle—because God looks on the heart!

Happily, in our consideration of this Corinthian letter, we are arriving at the junction of the 3rd and 4th chapters. It is there that the Apostle Paul explained the experience of "beholding the glory of the Lord," by which we are "transformed" into the image of Christ "from one degree of glory to another." This is very certainly a miracle—a direct work of God—for, as Paul states plainly, "this comes from the Lord who is the Spirit" [2 Corinthians 3:18]. As we will see for ourselves in Chapter 6, this miracle of "beholding" the Lord's glory brings about the spiritual reality for which David prayed: that is, to see the face of God! So, as Paul admonished another church, let us "press on toward the goal for the prize of the upward call of God in Christ Jesus" [Philippians 3:14]. As we do so, let's be hoping for a miracle.

---

11 "Joe Versus the Volcano," Warner Brothers, 1990. (This is the movie that Tom Hanks and Meg Ryan seem never to admit that they starred in.)

Chapter 6. THE FACE OF CHRIST

in which we see how that *face can change everything*

For God, who said, "Let light shine out of darkness," has shone in our hearts to give the light of the knowledge of the glory of God in the face of Jesus Christ.
[2 Corinthians 4:6]

In what we know as the "Sermon on the Mount," Jesus discloses the alarming words he will one day say to "many" people:

> On that day, many will say to me, 'Lord, Lord, did we not prophesy in your name, and cast out demons in your name, and do many mighty works in your name?' And then will I declare to them, '<u>I never knew you; depart from me, you workers of lawlessness</u>.'
> [Matthew 7:22,23]

Glory in the Face

In my preaching, I have read aloud that 11-word sentence many times. I have heard the words read by others. But I have a hope that I will never hear the Lord Jesus say them to *me*. "My hope is built on nothing less than Jesus' blood and righteousness." For that reason, I am not worried. This hope of mine has a good foundation. The blood and righteousness of Jesus is not sinking sand; and Christ himself—Christ alone—is solid rock.

On the other hand, I *can* imagine hearing the Lord Jesus say to me—in a somewhat similar (but less terrible) vein: "By my blood and righteousness, you *have* been saved from eternal punishment. By my grace, you *have* known me. But you have not known me *as well as you might have*." Less terrible, yes—but still, to be avoided, whatever the cost. Less terrible—but not out of the realm of dreadful possibility: everlastingly dreadful possibility.

In my first few years of living as a Christian, I took my new faith very seriously. Under the good influence of several believers more mature than I, I managed to develop, and to consistently practice, a number of beneficial spiritual disciplines. I learned to read the Bible regularly, to study books of the Bible inductively, to memorize strategically a series of Bible verses, to pray in an organized fashion, to resist and (on a good day) to overcome the temptations of the world, the flesh and the devil, and to communicate the gospel by drawing, and explaining, a simple illustration. I could feel the benefits of these new disciplines. And I thought I could see their good effects in my daily life.

In my opinion, the most beneficial (or "profitable"—as my new friends would say) was the discipline of memorizing Bible verses. It turned out that I was quite good at it. "Scripture memory" became "my thing." (Back in the 1970's, a person was pretty much *expected* to have a "thing.") I was steadily growing in my faith, and in my relationship with God, and I was very pleased with my new life.

Looking back at those happy days, I can see how my new spiritual disciplines corresponded to the first two answers to our

PRACTICAL QUESTION. My Bible reading and Bible study, by which I was learning many things *about* Jesus, aligned with the first answer to the QUESTION—and with the call in John 5:39 to "search the Scriptures" that "bear witness" about Jesus, as we saw in Chapter 2.

As I got the hang of fighting temptation (to a great degree, by an intentional focus on, and application of, my "memory verses"), I became more successful in my attempts to obey the commandments of the Lord consistently, which, of course, was the whole point of our QUESTION's second answer—and of John 14:21. I made no claim, in those early days, to be some sort of young male version of Mary Poppins—"practically perfect in every way"—and I caught myself quite regularly falling below my own ideas of the acceptable moral standards of a serious disciple of Christ. But still, I did feel that I was getting to know Christ, and that I was making progress in my allegiance to him. I was very pleased to be a Christian. I had lots for which to be thankful. It was the 1970's. I was young and healthy and happy. I had a terrific girlfriend—and we had lots to look forward to.

Then I read a famous sermon that C.S. Lewis had preached at a church in Oxford, England, in 1941. It was entitled *The Weight of Glory*, and it contained a six-word statement that really made me think. "We are far too easily pleased," the great man had said. It was *C.S. Lewis* who said those words. Was he not almost always right about *everything*? "For crying out loud!" I said to myself (as I was known to do in those days). "*He* invented Narnia. He wrote 'The Ransom Trilogy'—and 'The Screwtape Letters'! But was he right about *this*? Was he right about *me*? *Should* I be as pleased with my life as I am? As I said, the statement really made me think. Perhaps I was being sabotaged by what he called, in his autobiography, "the talent for happiness."[12]

---

12 The phrase appears in *"Surprised by Joy."* Twice in the first paragraph, in fact. Published by Geoffrey Bles, 1955.

It seemed to me that I *did* have that talent. Of course, I knew that, in itself, being good at being happy was not a bad thing. But *was* I too happy? *Had* I become happy too easily? My concern intensified. Might I be missing something of great importance? And was I missing it—whatever *it* was—without even noticing?

By the mercy of God, I was rescued from my uncertainty by Jonathan Edwards. In the early 1980's, I came across a sermon he had preached to his Northampton, Massachusetts congregation in the summer of 1733. It had made a very big first impression. The following year, it was published by "some of the hearers," for whom I am grateful to God. From that one sermon, I learned what it *was* that I might be missing—and how to know if I were.

There is more to knowing Christ than learning the Bible and living in consistent obedience to his commandments. As foundational and important as both those practices are, Jonathan Edwards knew of our essential need for something more, which he identified, in the title of his sermon, with his characteristic preference for lucidity over pithiness:

> *A Divine and Supernatural Light*
> *Immediately Imparted to the Soul by the Spirit of God,*
> *shown to be both a Scriptural and Rational Doctrine.*[13]

Not a pithy title at all, but very lucid. Except that now, almost three centuries later, more lucidity is required. For starters, when Edwards spoke of a "light" being "immediately imparted to the soul," he did not mean that it is imparted "right away." Rather, he meant that this "light" is imparted "without the use of any means that operate by their own power, or a natural force." In other words, this "divine and supernatural light" is imparted to a person without

---

13 Appendix I of this book is an outline of the sermon, with headings and subheadings in Edwards' own words.

any *other* person, or thing, serving as a mediator between the Spirit of God, who does this work, and the person being worked on.

Edward's popular sermon began with a brief explanation of what Jesus said in response to Simon Peter's spontaneous statement of belief. Peter had said, "You are the Christ, the Son of the living God." Jesus replied, "Blessed are you, Simon Bar-Jonah! For flesh and blood has not revealed this to you, but my Father who is in heaven" [Matthew 16:13-17]. To Edwards, these words of Jesus confirmed his sermon's "DOCTRINE":

> That there is such a thing as a spiritual and divine light, immediately imparted to the soul by God, of a different nature from any that is obtained by natural means.

In other words, just as God, the Father of Jesus, personally, and supernaturally, revealed to Peter the true identity of Jesus, so God himself directly imparts to some people a "spiritual and divine light." Only by this enlightenment, directly received from God, is anyone ever enabled to "see" what otherwise will remain unseen: that is, the true nature of God.

Following Edwards' usual practice, sub-headings of the sermon, four of them in *this* sermon, state succinctly both what this "supernatural light" is—and what it is not.[14]

> *What this spiritual and divine light is NOT*
> 1) It does not consist in any impression made upon the imagination.
> 2) It is not the suggesting of any new truths or propositions not contained in the Word of God.

---

14 This numbering of the subheadings is mine, not Edwards'.

What this spiritual and divine light IS
1) A *true sense* of the divine and superlative excellency of the things of religion: a real sense of the excellency of God and Jesus Christ, and of the work of redemption, and the ways and works of God revealed in the gospel.
2) There arises from this sense of divine excellency of things contained in the Word of God, *a conviction of the truth and reality* of them.

According to Mr. Edwards, this spiritual enlightenment is not the result of impressions made upon the imagination, or of suggestions of new knowledge from non-biblical sources. Rather, it is "a real sense" of the true excellence of God—Father, Son and Holy Spirit—*and* a sense of the excellence of the works and ways of God, especially his work of redemption. With this new sense—this new taste; this sight[15]—of how excellent a being God actually is, a person receives "a conviction of the truth and reality" of the "things contained" in the Bible. In other words, this "spiritual and divine light" directly empowers us to perceive that God is much more magnificent than we would otherwise ever know. This God-given enlightenment convinces us, as nothing else can, that what is stated in the Bible about God, and about the things of God—all that the prophets and the apostles have written—is actually true. In summary, this "light" is a sense and a conviction about the glorious nature of God.

As Edwards proceeded with his sermon, progressing from what Jesus spoke to Peter to what the Apostle Paul wrote to the Corinthians, he used the word "sense" 21 times—always as a noun; never as a verb—and always as a way of understanding what Paul meant by "beholding the glory of the Lord" [2 Corinthians 3:18].

---

15 Edwards frequently interchanged these metaphoric terms.

Similarly, Edwards chose the word "excellency" (and its plural) as a synonym for the Apostle's word "glory." His choice of these words clarifies his understanding of this "immediate" work of God depicted by Paul.

In other words, in the opinion of one especially brilliant, 18th century, New England preacher, the Apostle Paul's phrase, "beholding the glory of the Lord," means receiving, directly from God, a convincing perception of the unique excellence of God. Similarly, by the words "being transformed into the same image from one degree of glory to another" [2 Corinthians 3:18], the Apostle meant the experience of becoming increasingly *like* God in regard to all of the aspects of his being, and nature—all of them that can be possessed, to a degree, by a human being.[16]

In the same way, Edwards understood Paul's statement, that God has "shone in our hearts to give the light of the knowledge of the glory of God in the face of Jesus Christ" [2 Corinthians 4:6], to mean that God himself personally delivers, to some people— perhaps otherwise entirely ordinary people—an overwhelming and convincing sense of how incomparably excellent and glorious God is, by empowering them to "see" for themselves the character of Jesus.

This, I realized, might be the very thing I was missing. And without even knowing it! It seemed very likely. Being as pleased as I was with what I already had, and having not even heard of this mysterious, miraculous enlightenment, missing out on it was a very probable thing.

---

16 Theologians distinguish between the character traits of God that can be (to some imperfect degree) humanly possessed (e.g. His mercy, His justice) and those traits that cannot be (e.g. His omnipotence, His immutability), and refer to them, respectively, as the communicable and the incommunicable attributes of God.

But now that I *did* know about this shining "light," the pressing question was whether or not I *had* experienced it? By this time, I had been living in intentional submission and obedience to God for ten years. Imperfectly, of course; but it did seem to me that my God-given intentions to live for him, and serve him, were generally succeeding in overcoming my inborn carnality, my casually cultivated worldliness, and, of course, my "talent for happiness." So then, *had* God shone this light in my heart? *Had* I "immediately" received from God that convincing sense of his excellence?

Continuing my studying of Scripture, and my reading of the works of my Nine Dead men, I began to conclude that, in the last three years or so, God *had* been altering my understanding of him, and also the desires of my heart. These alterations, I thought with hindsight, had prepared me for the direct work of God that this one Edwards sermon explained: God's own supernatural shining in my heart of "the light of the knowledge of the glory of God in the face of Jesus Christ." As I continued to reflect on these interior changes to my understanding, I could see that my love and adoration for God, and for his Son, *had* intensified. Exactly when God shone this light in my heart, I had no idea. But that it *was* shining now seemed to me more and more obvious.

A part of this growing new certainty came from recalling how my increasing love for God, and for Jesus, had been showing up in "casual" conversations. I remembered theological debates (perhaps arguments and quarrels are the more accurate terms) that took place with other young pastors at denominational events. I sometimes found myself—often shoulder-to-shoulder with one or two like-minded colleagues—defending the reputation of God in regard to certain biblical texts that "our opponents" were suggesting were not to be taken too plainly. Their problem with these passages seemed to be the apparent depiction of God as unloving; as if God were an ill-tempered, mean-spirited, vindictive and tyrannical being. I recalled saying to them (or, in some circumstances, imagining saying to them), "Yes, yes! What you want to know is

The Face of Christ

just *who* God thinks he is!" Sometimes, I took an additional verbal step: "And I say 'Good for God'! He is God!! He can do what he pleases.'"

I probably did my reputation no good—tearing down rather than building relational bridges. But however indelicately (and therefore offensively) I presented my views, and revealed my heart, I *was* speaking in defense of the honour and holiness of God—the great and glorious God of heaven and earth; and of Jesus, the Son of God, the Word of God, my Saviour. I had come to love and adore God with my whole heart—and with all my soul and mind. And I was beginning to love my God with all my strength!

The conviction I reached was that during the previous three years of God-centred reading, study and learning, my heart *had* been enlightened. God *had* shone in my heart "the light of the knowledge of the glory of God in the face of Jesus Christ." With great joy, with heartfelt gratitude, and with a very real sense of relief, I began to believe that I hadn't missed it after all!

As for Jonathan Edwards, I thank God for his works, and for his life. With the help of his teaching, and from his account of the experiences by which his mind and heart had been transformed, I decided that, although he died almost 200 years before I was born, *he* was my man.[17]

Perhaps, more appropriately, I should have said that I was now one of *his*. For the next seven (or so) years of my pastoral life, Mr. Edwards was my most faithful tutor and guide, in the category of Dead Men. That is why, for all the years I have framed, and hung

---

17 I'm thinking of his diary, which can be found (online) in the biography at the beginning of Volume I of the two-volume collection of his "Works." Excerpts from his account of the "immediate" work of God in his own heart are included in this book's Appendix II.

on my walls, the portraits of certain dead men, *his* has always been among them.

There probably never has been a pastor or theologian less likely than Jonathan Edwards to neglect the Apostle Paul's mention of "the face of Jesus Christ." Edwards had as complete and comprehensive an adoration of the magnificence of Christ as anyone I have come across, in person or in print, dead or alive. As R.C. Sproule wrote in the foreword to a published collection of Edwards' sermons, "Here was a man whose heart was aflame with love and devotion for the sweetness and excellence of Christ."[18]

Edwards surely understood that what Paul explained in 2nd Corinthians 3 and 4 about this convincing, God-given sense of the unique excellence of God had everything to do with "seeing" the face of Jesus Christ.

Once I had concluded that I *had* received this sense and conviction, I found myself looking for it, and seeing it, in the lives of others. While I was still an assistant pastor in Toronto, I spoke to a young woman who took the time to tell me of her recent spiritual experience. She had been well raised in a happy Christian home. Since childhood, she considered herself as sincere a believer in Jesus as she knew how to be. Recently, though, she had been reconsidering her relationship with Christ. She described to me the personal effect of her participation in the Bible Study discussion group she had been leading. Somewhere in the middle weeks of the study, she told me, she observed a new sort of intensity in her love for God, and for Jesus. This reconsideration had raised a suspicion in her mind that she had only *recently* begun to believe in Christ; that only now—and not until now—she had become a "new creation"

---

18 *"Altogether Lovely: Jonathan Edwards on the Glory and Excellency of Jesus Christ."* Soli Deo Gloria Publications. A division of Ligonier Ministries, Inc. Orlando, Florida. 1997.

in Christ [2 Corinthians 5:17]. Perhaps her suspicion was correct. But Mr. Edwards, if *he* had been the Assistant Pastor, might have suggested to her that it was during those recent Bible studies that God himself had imparted to her his "divine and spiritual light"— that for many years she *had* been born again, but had not, until just recently, acquired a "sense" of the surpassing excellence of God and his Son.

More recently, I met a man of longstanding and consistent devotion to Christ, who in the last few years, had begun to take seriously, and to study intently, the theology of the Reformation. He told me of learning to understand—and love—the doctrine of God's sovereignty. As a result, he had begun to delight in God's electing love, his particular redemption of those for whom Christ specifically died, and the grace by which Christ provides, for his chosen ones, the desire and ability to persevere in their faith. The fruit of his diligent study had so changed his thinking about God, and the Lord Jesus, that he said he could best describe the experience as "being *born again* again"! He was aware, from his studies, that regeneration, by its very nature, is a once-in-a-lifetime experience. But still he felt as if he had recently undergone a *new* "new birth." The Apostle Paul, on the other hand, might have explained my new friend's recent transformation not as a more authentic regeneration, but rather as God himself enlightening his heart.

In my opinion, the explanation for both of these real-life changes—and for my own—is that, in all three cases, it was God "immediately" shining his supernatural light into our hearts. Surely, no one but God can light up a life the way he can. But both Paul the apostle and Edwards the pastor had helpful words to explain what happens whenever God does.

As for a third answer to the PRACTICAL QUESTION, is there some thing we can do to bring about this divine and spiritual "heart work" of God? A *simple* response would be "No." Someone could explain that there is nothing *to* do, beyond what we are instructed to do by the first two answers. It is true that, unlike the other answers, the third way of knowing Christ better is entirely an act of God, without anyone's mediation, or our initiative. Did not Paul himself write that this "beholding of the glory of the Lord ... comes from the Lord, who is the Spirit" [2 Corinthians 3:18]? But if we were to call this response *simplistic* rather than simple, we might see that there *is* something we can do. We can pray—perhaps as David did.

Throughout the long history of God's people, to "see the face of God" was to know him as intimately as is humanly possible. In the Psalms, David expressed his desire to know God intensely in several ways. He wrote of a longing "to gaze upon the beauty of the Lord" [Psalm 27:4], and of his desire to "look upon God in the sanctuary, beholding his power and glory" [Psalm 63:2]. But David also worded this desire as seeking God's face. Here are examples from two of the psalms labeled "Of David":

> Such is the generation of those who seek him,
> who seek the face of the God of Jacob. Selah
> [Psalm 24:6]

> Hear, O LORD, when I cry aloud; be gracious to
> me and answer me!
> You have said, "Seek my face."
> My heart says to you, "Your face, LORD, do I
> seek."
> Hide not your face from me ...
> [Psalm 27:7-9]

David, who God himself called "a man after my heart, who will do all my will" [Acts 13:22], *longed* to see God's face. Yet here in Psalm 27, in which he gives his fullest expression to this desire, David revealed his lack of confidence that such a wondrous privilege could ever be permitted. David's doubt had a history.

The Face of Christ

Centuries before David rose from his life as a shepherd to national leadership, Moses had travelled the same path [Exodus 3:1-6]. In his days of leading the nation of Israel, Moses specifically asked God for the same great privilege of knowing him personally. "Please show me your glory," he prayed [Exodus 33:18]. In reply, God said that he would respond to the request in two ways—but not in a third! God explained that he would, in the first place, make his goodness pass before Moses. Secondly, God said he would proclaim "before Moses" his name, which is "the Lord." But what God refused to do was to show Moses his face:

> "I will make all my goodness pass before you and will proclaim before you my name 'The LORD.' And I will be gracious to whom I will be gracious, and will show mercy on whom I will show mercy. But," he said, "you cannot see my face, for man shall not see me and live." And the LORD said, "Behold, there is a place by me where you shall stand on the rock, and while my glory passes by I will put you in a cleft of the rock, and I will cover you with my hand until I have passed by. Then I will take away my hand, and you shall see my back, but my face shall not be seen."
> [Exodus 33:19-23]

What God said to Moses is significant to anyone studying 2nd Corinthians 3, for there, the Apostle Paul plainly referred to Moses' experience with God. In the days of the Exodus, the people of God were not even able to look at the face of *Moses*, after Moses began to meet with God. This was the reason that Moses veiled his face.

> When Moses came down from Mount Sinai, with the two tablets of the testimony in his hand as he came down from the mountain, Moses did

Glory in the Face

not know that the skin of his face shone because he had been talking with God. Aaron and all the people of Israel saw Moses, and behold, <u>the skin of his face shone, and they were afraid to come near him</u>. But Moses called to them, and Aaron and all the leaders of the congregation returned to him, and Moses talked with them. Afterward all the people of Israel came near, and he commanded them all that the LORD had spoken with him in Mount Sinai. <u>And when Moses had finished speaking with them, he put a veil over his face</u>.

Whenever Moses went in before the LORD to speak with him, he would remove the veil, until he came out. And when he came out and told the people of Israel what he was commanded, the people of Israel would see the face of Moses, that the skin of Moses' face was shining. And <u>Moses would put the veil over his face again,</u> until he went in to speak with him.
[Exodus 34:29-35]

By contrast, Paul explained that, "we all," as the people of Christ, are privileged to behold the glory of the Lord with our faces *uncovered*—and *will* live to tell of it. But more than that, Paul wrote, we will be personally transformed by the experience:

> The Israelites could not gaze at Moses' face because of its glory ... [But] we are very bold, not like Moses, who would put a veil over his face ... And we all, with unveiled face, beholding the glory of the Lord, are being transformed into the

same image from one degree of glory to another.
For this comes from the Lord who is the Spirit.
[2 Corinthians 3:7-18]

If an interested onlooker, preferably one with both a background in biblical history and access to a reliable Time Machine, was able to contrast and compare the experience of Moses and the people of the Old Testament to the experience of Paul and the people of the New Testament, that onlooker might think to ask a question. How could such a different experience be possible for Paul and his people? It is a great and important question to ask. The stunning answer, as revealed by the Apostles, is that God had planned this great change from the very beginning.

The book of Acts records a prayer offered to God by his New Testament people. They prayed it not long after the death and resurrection of Christ. This prayer described the marvellous thing that was accomplished on the day we call Good Friday:

> "Sovereign Lord, who made the heaven and the earth and the sea and everything in them … truly in this city there were gathered together against your holy servant Jesus, whom you anointed, both Herod and Pontius Pilate, along with the Gentiles and the peoples of Israel, to do whatever your hand and your plan had predestined to take place."
> [Acts 4:24-28]

The spectacular and glorious truth is that the hideous abuse of Jesus Christ, in the events leading up to, and continuing for the duration, of his crucifixion, was the centrepiece of the plan that God had determined before the creation of the world. In his infinite and eternal wisdom, God had planned the permanent acquisition of the unspeakable human privilege of personally knowing God. According to his everlasting mercy and kindness, God granted to humanity, through the death and resurrection of Jesus, the privilege of experiencing what had previously been forbidden: the honour of knowing him, or, as David described it in the Psalms, of seeing God's face. This altogether unique change in humanity's relationship to God came about by God becoming "flesh" and living, physically, among the people of God [John 1:14].

While God was living among us—as one of us—great crowds of men and women heard about him, looked for him, found him, and heard him as he taught. They marvelled at what they heard, for his words were weighty, and powerful, and, by them, their hearts were pierced. He spoke unlike any rabbi they had ever heard. Not even the scribes spoke with such authority [Matthew 7:28,29]!

As the people stood before him, face to face, and listened, he said to them:

> "The Son of Man must suffer many things and be rejected by the elders and chief priests and scribes, and be killed, and on the third day be raised."
> [Luke 9:22]

He told them this repeatedly, but most who heard his words did not understand—and some who thought they *did* understand thought it impossible to believe. But what he said was true. In time, all he had prophesied took place exactly as he said. His rejection, suffering, execution, burial, resurrection: every one of his predictions was fulfilled.

And then, forty days after he had risen from the dead, Jesus left the people he called his friends [John 15:13-15]. Those who now believed in him; who now trusted him enough to obey him, he left. He ascended to the right hand of God. Ten days later, as Jesus had promised, the Holy Spirit of God came upon them, and dwelt within them, empowering them. In *that* strength, and in obedience to Christ, they went out into the world, as he had commanded them:

> "All authority in heaven and on earth has been given to me. Go therefore and make disciples of all nations, baptizing them in the name of the Father and of the Son and of the Holy Spirit, teaching them to observe all that I have commanded you. And behold, I am with you always, to the end of the age."
> [Matthew 28:18-20]

To this day, like-hearted people are still going, getting the good news out to those who have still not heard, and telling of their own new life as slaves, and friends, of Jesus. Whenever they go, Christ strengthens them to live out, and to explain, the unspeakably great privilege of really knowing God.

Now that Jesus is seated in majesty at the right hand of his Father; now that the Spirit of Christ dwells within every church of Christ—and in the heart of every Christian, we who know God through faith in Christ can see his face with spiritual eyes, or with "the eyes of our hearts" [Ephesians 1:18]. We can know him as well as if we were regularly talking with him, face to face. The human problem of being unable to know God—of being forbidden to see God's face—has been addressed. And it has been permanently resolved.

There *is* a third answer to the PRACTICAL QUESTION. There *is* something we can do, thirdly, **to know Christ better, and so be strengthened to face every challenge of life.** We can pray—as we often think to do—when we find that we need something that only God can provide. We can pray for God to show us his glory, as Moses did, but expecting a better answer. We can pray to see God's face, as David did, but with a clearer, better hope. We can **pray to see the face of Jesus Christ**, in the sense to which the Apostle Paul was referring when he wrote to the Corinthians of God's direct illumination of our hearts:

> For God, who said, "Let light shine out of darkness," has shone in our hearts to give the light of the knowledge of the glory of God in the face of Jesus Christ.
> [2 Corinthians 4:6]

As the difference between knowing *about* someone and getting to know him or her *personally* can be compared to the difference between biographical research and frequent telephone calls, so the difference we can pray for, according to the third answer, can be compared to you and that generous billionaire celebrity upgrading your friendship from phone calls to coffee dates.

There is nothing quite like a face to face conversation. Only with *that* sort of interaction can you convey to one another an "immediate" sense of what you are both thinking and feeling: by what you say, and also by the manner, and the mannerisms, with which you say it. As the two of you talk, there in the coffee shop face to face, you both are greatly assisted in your understanding of each other by the way in which you move your heads, your eyes and eyebrows, and your mouths and lips. Speaking regularly to one another, you learn one another's reactions and responses, even the slight, subtle and non-verbal ones. After many such conversations, you arrive at a greater level of mutual understanding than ever. And if you continue to grow in your love and respect for each other, you begin to love the same things, and to hate the same things. In time, you and your famous friend notice that the two of you now remind yourselves of one another.

That improbable sort of relationship is—to a degree—what the Apostle's mention of the face of Jesus Christ is all about. As God shines in our hearts that "light of the knowledge of his glory," we gain an increasing sense of how uniquely excellent he actually is. The more of God's greatness we sense, the more clearly we really "see" this divine being whom we have begun to love, to serve, and to worship. The more we come to know him, the more we are transformed into his likeness, which is to say: into conformity to Jesus, "the image of the invisible God" [Colossians 1:15]. And the more we become like Christ, the more we become strong—in "the strength of his might" [Ephesians 6:10].

The 17th century's John Owen brilliantly affirmed the connection of peace and strength to a personal knowledge of Christ, perhaps most clearly in the treatise known as *"The Glory of Christ."* Referring specifically to 2nd Corinthians 4:6, Owen wrote:

> By beholding the glory of Christ by faith, we shall find rest for our souls. Our minds are apt to be filled with troubles, fears, cares, dangers, distresses, ungoverned passions and lusts. By these, our thoughts are filled with chaos, darkness and confusion. But where the soul is fixed on the glory of Christ, then the mind finds rest and peace …

Not only through his diligent study of the Scriptures, but through his own bitter experience, Dr. Owen learned about "rest and peace" in times of "chaos, darkness and confusion". He and his wife had eleven children. But only one of the eleven, a daughter, lived to adulthood. Following the unhappy dissolution of her marriage, she too predeceased her parents. Shortly after *her* death, Owen's wife also died. He was left, at the age of 60, the sole surviving member of a family of 13. Yet just six years later, as he himself was dying of his many longstanding and painful physical ailments, he wrote confidently of "the rest for our souls" to be experienced by "beholding the glory of Christ by faith." His soul was "fixed on the glory of Christ," and his mind found "rest and peace."

Our relationship with the living Lord Jesus Christ is unique, because he is *altogether* unique. In every way, he is the superior

One: "in his being, wisdom, power, holiness, justice, goodness, and truth." Infinitely, eternally and unchangeably, Jesus Christ is perfect.[19]

So the more intimately we know Christ, the more we will wholeheartedly love him. And our respect for him will blossom into that deeply-rooted, divinely-empowered reverence, which is called, in the Scriptures, "the fear of God"—"the beginning of knowledge," "the beginning of wisdom," and "a fountain of life" [Proverbs 1:7; 9:10; 14:27].

So we should pray. Let us pray that our great and gracious God will enlighten us with the knowledge of his glory. Let us expect that as he does, we will, again and again, be overwhelmed by that "sense" and "conviction" of how thoroughly God surpasses all other beings in the excellence of his "greatness and power and glory and victory and majesty" [1 Chronicles 29:11]. And let us pray that we will be appropriately undone—and then remade—by that unique excellence, as it is reflected "in the face of Jesus Christ."

The Apostle Paul is our witness, with Owen and Edwards also bearing testimony, that, as God answers our prayer, we will be strengthened to face anything—and everything—as the people who have seen the face of Christ, for his face is "like the sun shining in full strength" [Revelation 1:16]. Let us believe that, whatever our circumstances, the face of Jesus Christ will keep us strong—and on the march, one deliberate, peaceful, joyful step at a time.

---

19 From the *Westminster Shorter Catechism*, (Question 4).

A PRACTICAL QUESTION:

What can we do to know Christ better and so be strengthened to face anything?

"Who are you, Lord?"

1. Learn as much about Christ as we can from diligent reading and study of the Bible. (John 5:39)

"What shall I do, Lord?"

2. Identify the commandments of Christ and live in consistent obedience to them. (John 14:21)

Anything else to do?

3. Pray that God will enable us to see the face of Christ. (2 Corinthians 4:6)

Chapter 7. IN THE FACE OF DEATH

with the strength to face the final enemy

We are always of good courage. We know that while we are at home in the body we are away from the Lord, for we walk by faith, not by sight.
[2 Corinthians 5:6,7]

Learning that I had caught a nasty case of terminal cancer was a great and sudden surprise to me only because the doctor who found it assumed that I already knew. But I didn't. All I knew was, that for the previous five months, I had been experiencing significant troubles in my, um, basement, and had therefore been spending more and more time in the three smallest rooms in the house. The doctor thought that he, his colleagues, and their tiny little camera, were simply checking out the *extent* of the cancer. In the middle of the procedure, he casually mentioned, "We're taking so *many* biopsies today just because you have so *much* cancer."

That was the first I had heard of it. "Really?" I said—meaning two things, because of the two questions that had just come to mind.

Primarily, I meant, "*Really*? I have *cancer*?" The answer, of course, was, "Yes!"—as in "Everyone knows that." But that wasn't actually true. I also meant, "*Really*? That's how you tell people they have *cancer*?" Here, the correct answer was, "No," but the man with the tiny camera didn't say a thing. In his mind, I suppose, the answer to the first question was too obvious for words. As for my second question, he didn't know that I didn't know.

A bit later, Deb and I were sitting alone in a large empty room, waiting to get what that doctor had to give: information, explanations and suggestions about what should be done first—and what could be done after that. We had just a few minutes to orient ourselves to the sobering surprise that we were now one of *those* married couples: the kind with one spouse sick enough to die sometime soon, and the other about to be widowed. Strangely perhaps—but in a good way—neither of us was inclined to deny what I had been told, or to take the position that there *must* be some sort of mistake. (It was not at all likely that a mistake had been made. It was *my* basement that the man's tiny camera was inspecting when he said what he had said.) Deb and I were both quite ready to hear what was going to happen next; and we were quite clear that it was our job to accept the news.

Minutes later, we learned that the first thing to do was to meet with two oncologists; to talk to one about radiation, and the other about chemotherapy. Of course, we did. From these doctors, one week later, we received a six-part plan: three chemotherapies (the first with radiation), and three surgeries; all to be scheduled over the next 18 months. When we asked the doctors to speak plainly, they said that *No*, this was not an early-detection story; that *Yes*, it was Stage IV cancer; that, *Actually*, if the plan was going to work, each one of the six parts had to go really, really well; and that, *By the way*, further complicating things was the 90% probability that I wouldn't live long enough to complete the 18-month plan. That sobering conversation took place almost 3½ years ago now ("*Time, times and half a time*," as it says in the book of Revelation), and I am (for now) still alive—and still taking chemotherapy.

One thing we often hear from various people, with their various perspectives on the subject of dying, is that we both seem to be bearing up well. We generally respond by mentioning the peace of God guarding our hearts and minds (of which Paul, the apostle, wrote) [Philippians 4:6,7], and the joy of the Lord being our strength (of which Nehemiah, the "wall-builder," spoke) [Nehemiah 8:10]. Some of these wonderfully caring people simply accept what we are saying. Others—equally caring but, perhaps, less convinced—lean in a bit, and quietly ask, "But how are you *really* doing?" So we explain. What we have been experiencing, since the day I joined the "Cancer Club," is the strength to face each challenge that comes our way, and the faith to manage what almost certainly *will* come our way—the incoming trifecta of dying, death and widowhood. We understand that this strength is not a gift especially reserved for cancer patients and their loved ones. It is a gift from God that we have been receiving for all of the years we have been alive: including the three decades (more or less) that we have been "that church's pastor," and "that pastor's wife."

For all those years, I had the privilege and challenge of trying to be a good and faithful shepherd to some seriously sick sheep. Often, in the case of some of the women on that list, Deb joined me in my pastoral work—sometimes in a big way. What we saw again and again was that, whatever impact our pastoral attention may have had on them, *we* were both significantly inspired by the examples of some of them. Nobody does everything perfectly. But quite a few of these ailing people—some of them cancer patients—demonstrated great strength and peace, and even joy, through their entire experience. Some of them were able to maintain their quiet and gracious hold on the truth that dying is not the worst thing that ever happens; and the confidence in God to believe that, for people who live for Christ, death is not a disaster.

I do remember driving away from the homes of some of those brave souls, or from a hospital visit, and telling myself, "If I am ever *that* sick, I want to be *that* strong, and have *that* peace and joy." The fact is, the strength that is now God's timely gift to Deb and me was, in part, taught to us by the examples of those women and men. It was a privilege to be their pastor. Their faith and their courage are still God's gifts to us. We remember them, and, in our hearts, we honour them, as King Lemuel honoured that now-famously "excellent wife." Strength and dignity were their clothing, and they smiled at the future [Proverbs 31:25, NASB]. Some of them, most heroically, retained the strength and dignity to keep on smiling as their illness made its last few moves—and said, "Checkmate."

From what we have already read (in Chapter 1 of 2nd Corinthians, and Chapter 2 of this book), we might conclude that the Apostle Paul thought of death as the most dreadful of enemies. It does *seem* to be what he was thinking when he wrote of the affliction that he and Timothy had experienced in Asia:

> We were so utterly burdened beyond our strength that we despaired of life itself. Indeed, we felt that we had received the sentence of death ... [God] delivered us from such a deadly peril, and he will deliver us. On him we have set our hope that he will deliver us again.
> [2 Corinthians 1:8-10]

"Utterly burdened beyond our strength"? "We despaired of life itself"? "The sentence of death"? "A deadly peril"? The words suggest that Paul *did* view death and dying the way most people do. But people who *knew* Paul knew better. Although his letters reveal him to be a man with many reasons to be disappointed, or desperate, distressed, despondent and depressed—or all of the above—some very plain statements set us straight.[20] For example, Chapters 4 and 5 of 2nd Corinthians contain *these* encouraging words: "we do not lose heart ... we do not lose heart ... we are always of good courage ... we are of good courage."

These bold assurances were made as Paul was teaching the Corinthians how to think about the inevitable deterioration of their own physical bodies, and their own certainty of dying. In other words, in this letter we observe the strength of Paul's faith, and the inspiring confidence of his "inner man." It is very easy to conclude that he faced his own dying and death fearlessly. Paul never stated, or even implied, that death was the most dreadful enemy; or that dying is the worst experience. In his previous letter to the Corinthians, he called death "the last enemy to be destroyed" [1 Corinthians 15:26]. Not the most dreadful foe; merely the last one. And not a foe that does nothing but damage. God can be counted on to accomplish some good through the death of everyone of his people.

In the New Testament letter to the Hebrews, we can read the details of what Jesus specifically accomplished by dying. There it is explained that, "crowned with glory and honor because of the suffering of death," Jesus "by the grace of God," tasted "death for everyone," in order that "through death," he was able "to destroy the devil, the one who had the power of death." And he accomplished more than that! Jesus delivered "all those who through fear of death were subject to lifelong *slavery*" [Hebrews 2:9-15]. To this, we should all take a great, deep breath and say, "Wow!"

---

20 Isn't it remarkable how much we English-speakers require the letter "d" to explain that we are, in one way or another, somewhat "down"?

Glory in the Face

All of Paul's letters are vividly coloured with what, in 2nd Corinthians, he called "good courage." And we can see for ourselves that this courage was not the result of his skill in the art of denial. Paul's courage was plainly God-given. With God's help, Paul was quite prepared to face, without flinching, the brutal realities of his own dying and death. Additionally, God had given Paul another gift: the spiritual discernment to understand clearly the difference between "the things that are seen," which are "transient," and "the things that are unseen," which are "eternal." Paul wrote matter-of-factly about the contrast between our physical bodies, which he referred to as "our outer self" [in Greek, "the outer man"] and our spiritual selves, which he calls "the inner" [2 Corinthians 4:16-18]. This gift of discernment was *not* the only source of Paul's death-defying strength of heart, but it was—and is—one source.

Certainly, the Apostle Paul did not need special inspiration to grasp the reality of how fragile a body he had. His many beatings and lashings, the three shipwrecks he endured—to say nothing of his enemies' strangely unsuccessful attempt to stone him to death—had left their marks on his flesh [Galatians 6:17], but not on his spirit. Such was his mindset that, "all the more gladly," he exalted in his "weaknesses." And he told the Corinthians he was content with his weaknesses; and with the "insults, hardships, persecutions, and calamities" [2 Corinthians 12:9,10] that were for him—for many years—an almost routine part of a typical day in the marketplace.

Paul was clearly not daunted by his knowledge of the certain demise of his body. He knew that his "inner man" was being "renewed day by day," and he knew what glory awaited him on the last day [2 Timothy 4:8]. In relative terms, Paul's burdensome afflictions were "light" and "momentary." The future that awaited him, on the other hand, was a solid thing: a weighty thing. He called it the "weight of glory" [2 Corinthians 4:17].

Metaphorically, Paul pictured life in his mortal body as living in a tent—and not a tent of such quality that it would never need

In the Face of Death

replacing. He believed that in due time—once he was out of his body—he would be moving into a house; the sturdy sort of house that a sensible realtor would recommend. But this house was "not made with hands."

Paul believed that, when he finally *was* moved in to the house that was awaiting him, that is, his own physical body, resurrected, and made both imperishable and immortal [1 Corinthians 15:50-53], he would find it in excellent condition. It was "eternal in the heavens." Apparently, the house came with a rock-solid warranty, personally drawn up and certified by the Builder. Professionally trained as a tentmaker [Acts 18:1-3], Paul knew a lot about tents, including the fact that, all things considered, a well-built house is always a better place to live. But Paul was not focused on the superiority of his future digs. To him, the whole point of "moving" was to live in the presence of God. There, he knew, he would see Jesus himself—and not from a distance, but face to face.

Walking by faith and not by sight [2 Corinthians 5:7], Paul understood that for every faithful Christ-loving slave of God, for the entire duration of months and years we are "at home in the body, we are away from the Lord." Speaking on behalf of all who *do* love Jesus—or ever will—Paul stated that "we would rather be away from the body and at home with the Lord." And he explained that, "whether we are at home or away, we make it our aim to please him." Then, perhaps less confident about his readers' faith than he sounded, he added—as a wake-up call, I think—that we "must all appear before the judgment seat of Christ, so that each one may receive what is due for what he has done in the body, whether good or evil" [2 Corinthians 5:6-10].

Paul's point was that Christ's people should focus their lives on the Lord. Everything Paul experienced—pleasant, not so pleasant, and not at all pleasant—he evaluated in reference to Christ, and to the interests of Christ. He really was "content with weaknesses, insults, hardships, persecutions, and calamities"—and he remained clear that everything he endured was "for the sake of Christ." This is the man who wrote to one church that, for him, "to live is Christ." Following that bold statement of faith, he added another one: "to die is gain" [Philippians 1:21].

I am very glad to have learned all this from Paul. For I am a man whose doctors, and whose terminal cancer, continue to challenge each other to a lively game of chicken. When pressed, my doctors say it is *not* a game they are going to win. So I find Paul's comparison of his present tent to his future house emboldening. And Deb and I continue to be both inspired and strengthened by Paul. Throughout these years "in sickness and in health," his words have kept us clear-headed. And the story of his perseverance has encouraged us to stay in the parade, walking forward, a step at a time, in the strength of the Lord. Paul's life persuades us that the grace of God will always be enough. So we remain confident that "the God of hope will continue to fill us with all joy and peace in believing, so that by the power of the Holy Spirit we will abound in hope" [Romans 15:13].

A specific hope of ours is that, when the time comes, Deb will be sufficiently strengthened to face the ungallant thing I am going to do. In the healthy years, I always assured her that God, in his steadfast love for us both, would permit me the gentlemanly privilege of not dying first. Now it is clear that I spoke presumptuously. Almost certainly, *that* long-term plan of mine also, disappointingly, has been rejected. I still sometimes quote my second favourite *Peanuts* character. Charlie Brown also knew disappointment. At times, he just put his head down and said: "Rats." (To be fair, he also sometimes said, with greater theological significance, "Good grief.") But Job said words that are better to quote. "The LORD gave, and the LORD has taken away; blessed be the name of the LORD" [Job 1:21].

In the Face of Death

Regarding the unknown timing of my death, Deb and I are steadied by the words that Paul pulled together from the books of Isaiah and Hosea. In his previous Corinthian letter, he wrote:

> Death is swallowed up in victory.
> O death, where is your victory?
> O death, where is your sting?
> The sting of death is sin, and the power of sin is
> the law.
> But thanks be to God, who gives us the
> victory through our Lord Jesus Christ.
> [1 Corinthians 15:55-57]

Those two prophets, and that one apostle, although seeing "in a mirror dimly" [1 Corinthians 13:12], were in complete agreement with one another—and, of course, they got this right. Death *has* lost its sting. Death was *not* victorious. Death was swallowed whole by the spectacular victory of Christ. And *that* victory Christ shares with us.

We can assume that when Paul's "time of departure" approached [2 Timothy 4:6], he faced his "last enemy" without a flinch. As we wait for the time of *my* departure, Deb and I keep in mind what Paul, and the prophets, and all of the proclaimers of the gospel, had in mind:

> *Now available: a new and improved way to die!*
> *Don't miss out on this terrific upgrade.*
> *It's now sting-free!*

Chapter 8.   GLORY ON PARADE

> in which the parade marches on—and
> people on the sidewalks join in
>
> But thanks be to God, who in
> Christ always leads us in triumphal
> procession...
> [2 Corinthians 2:14-16]

To this day in Italy, very close to the ruins of the Coliseum in Rome, there stands the ancient Arch of Titus. Built in the second half of the first century, it commemorates the 70 A.D. military victory of the army of Rome over the city of Jerusalem. Engraved on the under-side of the Arch is a *bas-relief* sculpture depicting what was known in those days as a triumphal procession, or a triumph. The Latin word is *triumphus*. In Paul's day, more-or-less everyone in the Empire knew what a triumph was. So in his letter, Paul did not pause to explain what he was referring to when he wrote that "Christ always leads us in triumphal procession."

Because a triumph was the celebration of a military victory, joy was the order of the day. The victorious military commander rode through the streets of Rome in a four-horse chariot. He was crowned with a laurel wreath; clothed with a purple toga that was stylishly embroidered in gold; and accompanied by his officers and soldiers; all of them happily sharing his glory, and eagerly anticipating a share of the spoils of battle.

There was great joy in the streets! But joy was not the only noticeable emotion. Also marching in the parade were the officers and soldiers of the conquered army, and captured citizens and slaves from the defeated state: each of them now the property of Rome; each of them now a piece of the spoils. Every step brought the unfortunate marchers closer to their destiny: some sort of enslavement, almost certainly miserable—or some sort of execution, almost certainly painful and humiliating.

With a purpose, the Apostle Paul picked up on the contrasting experiences of a triumph's participants. In his metaphor, Jesus Christ is the conquering hero. It is *his* victory being celebrated. Traditionally, a triumph proceeded through the streets of Rome to the Temple of Jupiter, the god of the sky and the thunder. There, sacrifices were offered, for Jupiter was considered the king over all other gods. But Paul knew Christ as the triumphant conqueror. Formerly, his captives were citizens of this world, and slaves of sin. Once captured by Christ they were marched to the throne of God, to be presented to "the blessed and only Sovereign, the King of kings and Lord of lords, who alone has immortality, who dwells in unapproachable light, whom no one has ever seen or can see" [1 Timothy 6:15,16]. In his previous Corinthian letter, Paul wrote, "Then comes the end, when he delivers the kingdom to God the Father after destroying every rule and every authority and power" [1 Corinthians 15:24].

What is not clear in Paul's depiction of Christ's victory celebration is the status of those whom Christ leads, referred to as "us." Was Paul thinking of himself, and all Christians, as Christ's officers and soldiers, sharing in his victory? Or was he thinking of "us" as the captured prisoners of Christ; so many slaves to be sacrificed to God? The metaphor *is* ambiguous—and, it seems, intentionally so. All of us who have committed ourselves to Jesus are *both* the joyous, victorious soldiers of Christ *and* his conquered captives. We are *all* being led "through the streets" of this world in triumphal procession—Christ's own slaves *and* soldiers [Romans 6:17,18; Ephesians 6:10-13]!

Jesus, the gracious and generous king, gives lavish gifts to his people. As did some of Rome's military victors, Christ especially delights to gives his friends slaves: living gifts that keep on giving; conquered men, women, youth and children whose faithful labours would wonderfully benefit many households. And marvellously, as Paul knew by experience, the slaves themselves would be glad to serve. Surely no one knew better than Paul the joy and satisfaction of being a slave of Christ. But Paul's service to the people of Jesus did not begin with his voluntary enlistment. On the contrary, Paul was drafted! Evidently, he had been something of a "draft-dodger" for some time, but in the Lord's plan, Paul came to see clearly that being captured by Christ was not a calamity. On the contrary, it was good news! It was, in fact, the gospel.

The Lord Jesus Christ was "the captain" of his salvation [Hebrews 2:10, KJV]. Christ had conquered him, and then recruited him, as "his own" [Philippians 3:12]. Now belonging to Christ, Paul was freed from all his previous enslavements. From that time on, his experience proved that everything involved in his new life in the service of Christ—even the worst of his many hardships—was a privilege, and all things were being worked out for his good, through the power, the love and the wisdom of his benevolent new owner.

Because it pleased the Lord to do so, Paul was given, as a personal gift, to the churches of Christ. In Jesus' name, Paul was assigned to serve the churches specifically as an apostle, a person "sent out" to serve. This he explained to the church in Ephesus:

> Grace was given to each one of us according to the measure of Christ's gift. Therefore it says, "When he ascended on high he led a host of captives, and <u>he gave gifts to men</u>" ... he gave the apostles, the prophets, the evangelists, the shepherds and teachers to equip the saints for the work of ministry, for building up the body of Christ ...
> [Ephesians 4:4-16]

There was never any doubt in Paul's mind that he had been given by the Lord to his people in order to serve them as an apostle and a servant. So there he was, marching with gratitude and joy through the middle decades of the first century, happily transformed to serve the Lord's churches—that is, the Lord's people—the very people whom he once had persecuted.

To this day, the triumph of Christ continues, and people on the sidewalks continue to step off the curb and join in. In every case, before they ever decide to join the march—before it ever even occurred to them to do so—our great God, Father, Son and Holy Spirit, had committed himself to their transformation. Jesus explained this, telling his apostles, "You did not choose me, but I chose you and appointed you that you should go and bear fruit and that your fruit should abide ..." [John 15:16]. Speaking for all such chosen captives, Paul wrote, "Thanks be to God, who in Christ always leads us in triumphal procession ..."

Giving thanks to God is always a good thing to do, but the personal circumstances surrounding this expression of Paul's thanks are worth noticing. In the two previous sentences, Paul explains the backstory:

> When I came to Troas to preach the gospel of Christ, even though a door was opened for me in the Lord, my spirit was not at rest because I did

not find my brother Titus there. So I took leave of them and went on to Macedonia.
[2 Corinthians 2:12,13]

What Paul was revealing with these words was that, in addition to many other hardships, he was troubled by the Corinthians' response to a tough decision he had made; a decision that greatly increased their disrespect for him. By this awkward circumstance, his complicated relationship with them had further deteriorated. Intriguingly, it was specifically *this* hardship that prompted Paul to liken his life and ministry to a triumph:

> But thanks be to God, who in Christ always leads us in triumphal procession, and through us spreads the fragrance of the knowledge of him everywhere. For we are the aroma of Christ to God among those who are being saved and among those who are perishing, to one a fragrance from death to death, to the other a fragrance from life to life. Who is sufficient for these things?
> [2 Corinthians 2:14-16]

"The fragrance of the knowledge of Christ"? These words refer to what was "in the air" as a triumph walked by. There was always, of course, the smell of both humans and beasts. But there was also the aroma of burning incense and perfume. A triumph not only looked and sounded memorable: it *smelled* that way, too. But the aromas, like the sights and sounds, meant very different things to different marchers, for the marchers were people with different destinies. As the marchers were led to Jupiter's temple, there was joy *and* terror on the streets, with reactions to both emotions on the sidewalks.

The New Testament book of Acts tells us that, some time before his Damascus Road experience, Saul witnessed, and actually played a part in, the brutal death of Stephen, the first person ever to be killed for believing in Jesus Christ:

> And Saul approved of his execution. And there arose on that day a great persecution against the church in Jerusalem, and they were all scattered throughout the regions of Judea and Samaria, except the apostles.
> [Acts 8:1] (See also Acts 7:58)

Saul prominently participated in this first organized assault on the controversial new movement that people called "the Way." But who knows how God, in the months that followed, used Saul's continuing recollection of Stephen's death to chip away at his proud heart, and to wear him down in his unbelief. Perhaps the guilt of his participation in, and his own approval of, the killing of Stephen, was one of the "goads" that Paul found it hard to "kick against" [Acts 26:14]. Perhaps the stench of his memories was one of the means God used to convert him. God *is* able to turn a "heart of stone" into a "heart of flesh" [Ezekiel 36:26], and it seems that he does delight, at times, to bring about such transformations in unexpected, and even ironic, ways.

By the power of God, and to accomplish his "good and acceptable and perfect" will, the bad smell that our good works, at times, emit are used by God "in the nostrils" of people on the sidewalk. As we march by, God can give those people "ears to hear" what we say, and "eyes to see" us for what we are. Because of this happy possibility, we, as the Lord's slaves, are under strict orders to "not be quarrelsome but kind to everyone, able to teach, patiently enduring evil, correcting our opponents with gentleness, knowing that God can, and praying that God will, grant them repentance leading to a knowledge of the truth, that they may come to their senses and escape from the snare of the devil, after being captured by him to do his will" [2 Timothy 2:24,25].

As we march, we must understand that people can learn, from observing us, to sense for themselves—to smell the aroma—of the presence, and the essence, of the Lord. This happy possibility, in itself, should be enough to persuade us to count our trials as joy, as did Paul, and as did other members of the first-century church [James 1:2]. And we should know that *especially* in our difficulties, the joy of the Lord that strengthens us, and the peace of God that guards our hearts and minds, can be very noticeable. The Holy Spirit can use our peace and joy to inspire people to consider what they are noticing. Would it not be a very fine thing, someday, to be sought out and found by the very people who had once looked upon our devotion to Jesus with contempt? What a joy it would be to hear them explain how God changed their minds, making use, perhaps, of their memories of our kindness to them, and of our patience with them. Perhaps God *will* be pleased to convince them to step off the sidewalk and join us in the parade!

Whatever might be the personal reactions to the "fragrance" of our faith—whether people are attracted, or repulsed, by the lives we live in devotion to Christ—we *are*, according to Paul, "the aroma of Christ to God." Whether people's reactions are negative or positive—or even a confusing combination of both—we *must* "walk in a manner worthy of the calling to which [we] have been called" [Ephesians 4:1]. We must continue to believe that God will supply us with the strength we require to face anything. For our hearts are now shining with "the light of the knowledge of the glory of God in the face of Jesus Christ."

For every affliction; every changed circumstance; every person who is to us what Job's friends were to him, what Joseph's brothers were to him, and what some Christians in Corinth were to Paul, our great God's grace is sufficient, and always will be. His grace, and his gift of strength, will always be enough.

The parade continues. Up at the front, Paul and the other apostles have marched. Centuries later, the likes of Owen and Edwards followed faithfully in their steps. Behind them marched Spurgeon and Chesterton and Lewis. In these confused days of the 21st century, a long way behind those giants, some less-known, less-notable Christians are marching, too. Christians like me, for example—and perhaps like you. Many of us still have some distance to walk. But we are the captives of Christ: the recruited, equipped and grateful slaves of the most excellent owner and master of all time. And each of us is offered the strength of faith, and of character, to face what God sets in front of us.

What Paul wrote to the Christians living in Philippi, let us also take to heart. "Brothers, join in imitating me, and keep your eyes on those who walk according to the example you have in us" [Philippians 3:17]. As we do, let us keep our hearts focussed on the day when, at last, we will see our most glorious Lord Jesus, face to face—and just "as he is" [1 John 3:2].

I am now several years along the winding path of the "unhealthy" portion of my march. My plans for the future have all been dashed to pieces, and my circumstances continue to change. Month by month, I acquire new inconveniences and annoyances. And there are disappointments, physical challenges, and new medical strategies. Vocationally, I have said a quiet good-bye to pastoring a church. Personally, I have bidden a fond farewell to long-distance running, solo canoe trips, and many other things that I loved for a long time, but now have lost.

Along with these losses have come happy new opportunities. For a while, I have the time—and for now, at least, the energy—to write. And I have other new pleasures. For the first time in my adult life, I have *lots* of time for reading! But that is more than just a pleasure. It is also a great help to me in maintaining the state of heart and mind appropriate to a man with a really important upcoming appointment [Hebrews 9:27; 2 Corinthians 5:10].

Here I acknowledge my thanks to God for the life and writing of John Owen. For several years now, I have been reading and re-reading, with great faith-strengthening delight, two of his most Christ-focused works:

> "*Meditations and Discourses on*
> *THE GLORY OF CHRIST,*
> *in his Person, Office, and Grace:*
> *with the Differences between Faith and Sight;*
> *Applied unto the use of them that believe*"

which he wrote, in 1683, as he was dying(!)—and an equally brilliant treatise he had written four years before:

> CHRISTOLOGIA:
> *or, a Declaration of the Glorious Mystery of the Person of Christ—God*
> *and Man,*
> *with the infinite Wisdom, Love, and Power of God*
> *in the Contrivance and Constitution thereof;*
> *as also, of the Grounds and Reasons of his Incarnation;*
> *the Nature of his Ministry in Heaven;*
> *the Present State of the Church above thereon;*
> *and the Use of his Person in Religion,*
> *with an Account and Vindication of the Honor, Worship, Faith,*
> *Love, and Obedience due unto him, in and from the Church.*

As desperate times call for desperate measures, so important times call for important contemplation. The fruit of Dr. Owen's hard work has provided me with what seems exactly the right books to contemplate these days.

Happily, I also have time for re-connecting with friends and associates, some from years ago—and for staying close to a few friends, who I know will be an encouragement to me in the challenges I am going to face. Additionally, God has given me what some men never get: enough time to say a slow and thorough good-bye to my three adult children—and to my courageous, excellent wife.

Deb and I believe that *her* uncertain future is more daunting than my more certain one. But I say, as King Lemuel would—if only he had met her!—she is clothed with strength and dignity, and she trusts God to give her the strength to keep smiling.

The mercy and steadfast love that God has shown me for many years—in these last years especially—make me very eager not to mess this up. But I am confident that, by the faithfulness of Christ, as I abide in him, and as his Word abides in me [John 15:5,7], he *will* strengthen me—and "keep [me] from stumbling," to present me "blameless before the presence of his glory with great joy" [Jude 1:24]. "Because he is at my right hand, I shall not be shaken" [Psalm 16:8].

Deliberately imitating Paul, I dare say it is "my eager expectation and hope that I will not be at all ashamed, but that with full courage now as always Christ will be honored in my body, whether by life or by death" [Philippians 1:20]. And what King David sang to conclude the 17th Psalm, and to begin the 18th, I say to my glorious Lord Jesus:

> As for me, I shall behold your face in righteousness;
> when I awake, I shall be satisfied with your likeness.
>
> I love you, O Lord, my strength.

APPENDIX I

[An 800 word summary of the 8,700 word
sermon Mr. Edwards preached.]

A DIVINE AND SUPERNATURAL LIGHT, IMMEDIATELY IMPARTED TO THE SOUL BY THE SPIRIT OF GOD, SHOWN TO BE BOTH SCRIPTURAL AND RATIONAL DOCTRINE

Preached by **Jonathan Edwards** at Northampton, in 1733,
and published at the desire of some of
the hearers, in the year 1734.

Matthew 16:17

And Jesus answered and said unto him, Blessed art thou, Simon Barjona: for flesh and blood hath not revealed it unto thee, but my Father which is in heaven.

CHRIST says these words to Peter upon occasion of his professing his faith in him as the Son of God. Upon this occasion, Christ says as he does *to* him, and *of* him in the text: *in which we may observe,*

1. That Peter is pronounced blessed on this account.
2. The evidence of this his happiness declared;
that God, and he *only*, had *revealed it* to him.

First, As it shows how peculiarly favored he was of God above others.

Secondly, It evidences his blessedness also, as it intimates that this knowledge is above any that *flesh* and *blood* can *reveal.*

Positively, as God is here declared the author of it.

Negatively, as it is declared, that *flesh and blood* had *not revealed it.*

DOCTRINE: That there is such a thing as a spiritual and divine light immediately imparted to the soul by God, of a different nature from any that is obtained by natural means.

—And on this subject I would show,

I. WHAT THIS SPIRITUAL AND DIVINE LIGHT IS.

And in order to it, would show, *First,* **in a few things, what it is not.**

1. Those convictions that natural men may have of their sin and misery, is not this spiritual and divine light.
2. This spiritual and divine light does not consist in any impression made upon the imagination.
3. This spiritual light is not the suggesting of any new truths or propositions not contained in the Word of God.
4. It is not every effecting view that men have of religious things that is this spiritual and divine light.

Appendix I

Secondly, **positively what this spiritual and divine light is.**

1. A true sense of the divine and superlative excellency of the things of religion: a real sense of the excellency of God and Jesus Christ, and of the work of redemption, and the ways and works of God revealed in the gospel.
2. There arises from this sense of divine excellency of things contained in the Word of God, a conviction of the truth and reality of them; and that either ***indirectly or directly.***

Indirectly, in two ways:
1. As the prejudices that are in the heart, against the truth of divine things, are hereby removed; so that the mind becomes susceptive of the due force of rational arguments for their truth.
2. It not only removes the hindrances of reason, but positively helps reason.

APPENDIX II

FROM THE DIARY OF JONATHAN EDWARDS: his personal reflections on his personal discovery of "a sweet sense" of the sovereignty and majesty of God:

From my childhood up, my mind had been full of objections against the doctrine of God's sovereignty, in choosing whom he would to eternal life; and rejecting whom he pleased; leaving them eternally to perish, and be everlastingly tormented in hell. It used to appear like a horrible doctrine to me. But I remember the time very well when I seemed to be convinced, and fully satisfied, as to this sovereignty of God, and his justice in thus eternally disposing of men, according to his sovereign pleasure.

… But I have often, since that first conviction, had quite another kind of sense of God's sovereignty than I had then. I have often since had not only a conviction, but a *delightful* conviction. The doctrine has very often appeared exceedingly pleasant, bright, and sweet. Absolute sovereignty is what I love to ascribe to God. But my first conviction was not so.

Glory in the Face

...The first instance, that I remember, of that sort of inward, sweet delight in God and divine things, that I have lived much in since, was on reading those words, *Now unto the King eternal, immortal, invisible, the only wise God, be honour and glory for ever and ever. Amen* [1 Timothy 1:17]. As I read the words, there came into my soul, and was as it were diffused through it, a sense of the glory of the Divine Being; a new sense, quite different from any thing I ever experienced before.

... From about that time I began to have a new kind of apprehensions and ideas of Christ, and the work of redemption, and the glorious way of salvation by him. An inward, sweet sense of these things, at times, came into my heart; and my soul was led away in pleasant views and contemplations of them. And my mind was greatly engaged to spend my time in reading and meditating on Christ, on the beauty and excellency of his person, and the lovely way of salvation by free grace in him. I found no books so delightful to me, as those that treated of these subjects. Those words used to be abundantly with me, *I am the rose of Sharon, and the lily of the valleys.* [Song of Solomon 2:1]. The words seemed to me sweetly to represent the loveliness and beauty of Jesus Christ.

... Before, I used to be uncommonly terrified with thunder, and to be struck with terror when I saw a thunderstorm rising; but now, on the contrary, it rejoiced me. I felt God, if I may so speak, at the first appearance of a thunderstorm; and used to take the opportunity, at such times, to fix myself in order to view the clouds, and see the lightning play, and hear the majestic and awful voice of God's thunders, which oftentimes was exceedingly entertaining, leading me to sweet contemplations of my great and glorious God. While thus engaged, it always seemed natural for me to sing or chant forth my meditations; or, to speak my thoughts in soliloquies with a singing voice.

ACKNOWLEDGMENTS

The Bible says, "Faithful are the wounds of a friend…" [Proverbs 27:6]. I believe that. Faithful also are the literary criticisms, corrections and suggestions of friends who have the editorial chops and the spiritual wisdom to provide them. So here I acknowledge, and give thanks to God for, the very great help I have gratefully received from one new friend: **Carolyn Weber**; one recently re-acquired friend from my years in youth ministry: **Bruce Longenecker;** and one West London friend: **Ray Majoran**.

All three, published authors themselves, have generously given their valuable time and attention to my writing of this book—and have faithfully offered, in addition to many encouragements and kind words, their very good criticisms, corrections and suggestions; all in the most faithful but non-wounding ways. It never hurt at all. If books could talk, I am sure that this one would join me in thanking the three of them for helping it to become the best book it could be. For their great assistance, I will remain thankful for the rest of my life—although, admittedly, this is now a fairly easy commitment to make.

I also acknowledge the specific ongoing encouragement I have received from two good and faithful friends who have, from the start, maintained an active interest in this writing project. From both **Andy Whynot** and **Greg Wyton**, I have enjoyed, along with many cups of black coffee and good conversations, great strong encouragements to keep on writing. And I did.

On the topic of good friends, I must also acknowledge **Sunder Krishnan**; the man I refer to in this book as "my most faithful pastoral colleague." We met shortly after we had both been invited to join the pastoral staff of the Toronto churches where we worshipped. A significant portion of my philosophy of pastoral ministry was worked out in the conversation that Sunder and I have been having, and enjoying, for 3½ decades: a conversation as good as it has been long.

Finally, bringing my total of personal acknowledgements to seven—a very significant number, biblically—I thank God for **my wife, Deb.** In view of the man I have become, and the work that God gave me to do, she really has been "practically perfect in every way." Really! I could never fully express how much she has influenced, and upgraded, my life and my character. But I could start by explaining that my rejection of Linus Van Pelt's view of people (described in Chapter 4) was almost entirely the product of her influence. So was my actual adult commitment to an actual church. Besides all that, Deb has been, for these past few years, a most attentive and faithful amateur health-care provider—but never because she needed something more to do!

The Bible also says, "An excellent wife is the crown of her husband ... He who finds a wife finds a good thing, and obtains favor from the Lord" [Proverbs 12:4;18:22]. I believe that, too.

ENDORSEMENTS

"Finding the strength to face anything"! What qualifies someone to write a book that accomplishes such a formidable objective? For starters, *a command of the English language* so that the reading itself would be a pleasure. Secondly, *a well developed, truly biblical theology* since the source of the strength is God himself. Thirdly, *wisdom to apply the knowledge of God's character and ways* to the point where the proverbial rubber meets the road in the life of the reader. Fourthly and perhaps most importantly, *finding that very strength* to handle prolonged personal suffering without loss of faith and with grace. In my friend Mike Wilkins, these four strands have converged to produce the book that you now hold in your hands. It will remain one of my most treasured possessions, celebrating as it does, a blessed friendship that has lasted 33 years at the time of writing."

REV. SUNDER KRISHNAN served as the Preaching Pastor of Rexdale Alliance Church (in Toronto), from 1980-2016, and was its Senior Pastor since 1996. He is the author of several books, including *The Conquest of Inner Space: Finding Peace in a Chaotic World*, and *Hijacked by Glory: From the Pew to the Nations*.

"For more than four decades, Mike Wilkins has blessed many with his faithful, creative, engaging, and practical expositions of Scripture. His challenging and inspiring reflections in this book are no exception. Light-heartedly interspersing poignant musings on his own life (and his recent "fall from health") with skilled and masterful meditations on Scripture, Wilkins insightfully probes the deep theological soils of one of the apostle Paul's richest letters (2 Corinthians)."

Dr. Bruce W. Longenecker is Professor of Early Christianity and the Melton Chair of Religion at Baylor University (Texas). He is the author of a number of books, including *The Lost Letters of Pergamum* (Baker Academic) and *The Cross before Constantine: The Early Life of a Christian Symbol* (Fortress Press).

"With wit, humour, intelligence and wisdom, Wilkins shares his deep love for God with a poignancy that comes from a life lived earnestly to the glory of God. He does this with an illuminating nod to other spiritual thinkers who have helped him on this journey. Whether in joy or grief, contentedness or suffering, Wilkins' words remind us that God's glory permeates our broken world with intimations of hope for the restored one. In seeking God's face, we face nothing, not even death, alone. And in the seeking, nothing, not even death, is in vain."

Dr. Carolyn Weber is an award-winning author, speaker and professor. Her books include *Surprised by Oxford* (HarperCollins) and *Holy is the Day* (IVP).

ABOUT THE AUTHOR

Mike Wilkins was born in 1954, in Kingston, Ontario, but did most of his growing up 50 miles down the St. Lawrence River in the pretty little city of Brockville.

In 1973, Mike met his future wife, Debbie Street, when they were both 18 years old. What she liked about him was his quick wit, his thick blonde hair, his serious commitment to Christ, and his absolute disinterest in ever becoming a pastor. What Mike liked about her was basically everything.

Four years later, the month of May was big for Mike and Deb. In four short weeks, they graduated from Queen's University; Mike started a full-time job at a publisher of children's books; and they married each other.

"Life has a way of changing a man; and God has many ways," Mike writes. This explains why, in 1984, with two young kids—and hopes of a third one some day, Mike and Deb moved to London, Ontario, where Mike became the pastor of West London Alliance Church. For the 30 busy years he continued his ministry, Deb was Jessica, Ben and Joanna's stay-at-home mom, then their homeschool teacher, and then an employee of Compassion Canada, where, at the time of this writing, she still happily continues to work.

While he was a healthy adult, Mike's hobbies—in addition to child-raising—were long-distance running, canoe-tripping, reading (and re-reading) old books, and writing and directing plays that the church was pretty well forced to stage.

CPSIA information can be obtained
at www.ICGtesting.com
Printed in the USA
LVOW08s1455161216
517613LV00002B/426/P